Thunder & Mud

Beyond the Hour

Should some greedy power demand
A portion of life's memories,
I'd say take the laughs
But leave the tears.
From each sorrow I have learned
And remembering,
Learn again.

A broken doll
A friend untrue
A fortune lost
A child who stayed but a day.

Each in its way has taught me
To laugh, to cry
To love and ask not why.

Julia Brown Tobias

Thunder & Mud

A Pioneer Childhood
on the Prairie

Julia Brown Tobias

Illustrations by B.J. Durr
& Sue Kepros Hartman

High Plains Press

FIRST PRINTING

10 9 8 7 6 5 4 3 2 1

Library of Congress Cataloging-in-Publication Data

Tobias, Julia Brown
Thunder and mud : a pioneer childhood on the prairie / Julia
Brown Tobias : illustrations by B.J. Durr & Sue Kepros Hartman.
p. cm.
ISBN 0-931271-29-0
1. Tobias, Julia Brown, 1902- --Childhood and youth.
2. Pioneer children--Nebraska--Biography.
3. Girls--Nebraska--Biography.
4. Frontier and pioneer life--Nebraska.
5. Nebraska--Social life and customs.
6. Nebraska--Biography.
I. Title.
F656.T63 1995
978.2'031'092--dc20   95-41915
[B]   CIP

HIGH PLAINS PRESS
539 CASSA ROAD
GLENDO, WYOMING 82213

Dedicated to my family with love.

*Also, I wish to thank the members of my Writers' Group
who encouraged and advised me—
Linda Roggensack, Sue Leever, and
Sue Kepros Hartman, in particular.*

CONTENTS

The Years I Can't Remember

OR SOME REASON Mama never treated me like a child. She always said, "you and the children," never "you children." She never stopped what she was saying to grownups when I came into the room. In some way she communicated to me that in exchange for this relationship, I must always mind better and behave better than children did. On the occasions when I failed, I was scolded, spanked, or relieved of my privileges for a time.

I used to wish I could personally know the years between the time Mama and Papa met and the time my memory begins. Actually it was only nine or ten years, and so much of those years was revealed to me as Mama and I visited when working together, that I now sense those years almost as though I had lived them, although I have a sharp line between what I remember and what I was told.

Mama grew up as Erma Lowther in southern Ohio in woods and farm country. The Lowther family pioneered that area in the 1700s. Her education came from the local school and "subscription school." Subscription school is something I've never heard of in any other place. Someone qualified to teach high school would get permission to use the local schoolhouse during the summer and then get subscribers to his school. The teacher would dicker with a family as to how much they could or should pay for the courses their children were to be taught. Such schools bridged the difference between country schools and college for many students in that area.

The community offered little to young people when they finished school, so one by one, Mama's three brothers left home and headed west. Having an aunt and uncle in Nebraska made that a point of destination for them. When Mama wanted to follow her brothers to Nebraska, her mother said, "Only if you can live with your Aunt Jenny, as no daughter of ours is ever going out into the world alone." And she added, "What would people think?"

Mama wrote a letter to Aunt Jenny asking if she might come to live with her. In reply, her aunt wrote, "I will be glad to have you if you are willing to help me with my children and housework and will obey me as my own daughter. In exchange, you will receive enough for spending money and clothes and will live as one of the family. Life here is very different from Ohio. We have a large farm and many horses and cattle, therefore, we always have extra men to cook for. We work hard out here in Nebraska."

It was agreed that Mama could go to Nebraska as soon as she had someone to travel with. That spring, in 1898, a friend was going by train as far as Chicago. Grandma consented to Mama traveling alone from Chicago to Omaha where Aunt Jenny would meet her and take her to the farm near Plattsmouth.

Mama was only nineteen and, despite the long days that began at five in the morning and ended at ten at night, she loved the new life in Nebraska. There was always activity and people. Aunt Jenny and Uncle Louie were gay and happy. Their seven small children were like little brothers and sisters to Mama. They laughed when she said words like "a far piece" and "right smart," and she was quick to substitute words more acceptable in her new land. She learned other things too, such as how to cook for fifteen or twenty people, and still find time to wash,

iron, bake bread, and churn, as well as care for small children. It
was Aunt Jenny who taught Mama to sew so beautifully.

Shortly after Mama came to live with Aunt Jenny, she
began to hear about Charley Brown. Charley Brown was coming to train some of Uncle Louie Todd's trotting horses for the
race track. Even the children talked about what they would do
when Charley Brown came. Aunt Jenny talked about what
Charley Brown liked to eat and everyone talked about what he
could do with horses. Mama decided she'd heard enough of
Charley Brown, but that was before she met him, a tall, boyish
man with dark brown eyes that were the kindest eyes she had
ever seen, and a shy smile that crinkled about his eyes before it
reached his mouth. Charley Brown was everything they said and
more. There was only one place they were wrong. They said,
"Charley Brown never looks at girls. He will never get married
as he is too content at home."

Mama and Charley Brown were married the next spring
and there followed for them a carefree year of fun. They didn't
have a home of their own but spent part of the year with Grandpa and Grandma Brown, helping them with farm work and the
rest of the time with the horses.

Charley (whom I knew as Papa) trained horses both for
himself and Mama's uncle. He broke colts to harness and trained
them each to pull a racing sulky, a light-weight, two-wheel cart
on which the driver sat high and close behind the horse. The
trainer tried to get the very best from each horse. Some horses
made the best time by holding back at the start and finishing
fast. Others did better by holding a steady pace throughout the
race. Colts had to learn to give their best without ever breaking
from a trot, which would disqualify them from a race. Papa was
what was known as a natural horseman. He was kind to his
horses but demanded military-like obedience, and a horse was

fairly and humanely punished when he disobeyed. One of Papa's sayings was that "a horse and his driver must always be able to trust each other."

That year, 1898, was the year that Papa's big horse Eli won many races at the county fairs and the Nebraska State Fair. Papa loved to race but never bet. He said, "It ceases to be fun if you stand to lose anything more than the race."

Mama learned to drive spirited horses that summer. Papa found it unthinkable that anyone should be unable to handle a good horse. First Mama learned the basic rules, such as never lay down the reins when a horse is hitched to a rig of any kind. Always keep a tight rein and don't nag a horse. Give him just the orders you want obeyed and see that he does obey them. Then, giving Mama the reins, Papa said, "Trust your horse and he'll be glad to serve you." Mama found it to be true and, by that fall, she could take a horse any place she wanted to go. Her favorite was a little bay named Klondike.

The only flaw in the year was the relationship between Mama and Papa's only sister. Aunt Flo and Papa had been unusually close, and it had never occurred to her that she would ever share his time and attention. Unfortunately, Mama's worst fault was being overly possessive of those she loved. Sometimes Mama felt uncomfortable with her new family, as they were all better educated than she, and seemingly had read everything ever written. Even their jokes made reference to something from a book. Their conversation was frequently over her head, and she began to read and study with a will. In a few years, she could match wits with anyone in the family.

Grandpa Brown, the dreamer, was never aware of any friction, but Grandma saw in Mama a loyal, loving and capable wife for her beloved Charley. She did everything she could to help Mama learn the ways of the Brown family. Maybe she remembered some thirty-five years back when she moved from a Methodist preacher's home into the life of the Browns where everyone was a wild "reformer" and a "nonconforming intellectual." Grandma even explained some of it to Mama.

"Ermie," she said, "the Browns are all dreamers and they put everything they have into their dreams. You'll find yourself hating those dreams, yet believing in them, and fighting beside the dreamer. But one thing, Ermie, don't ever expect to have very much money. It just isn't important to the Browns."

The next year, Papa sold some of his horses and set up farming for himself some thirty miles from his parents' home. Mama loved having her own home and, buying a new sewing machine, she set to work preparing for her first child. He was born in October and was named William Talmage, after Papa's beloved older brother. The elder William Talmage had been an Episcopal minister who had been ordained in June and died the next September with typhoid fever. It had been a great tragedy in the Brown family.

The younger William Talmage was born for tragedy too, even sadder. He was what they then called "thyroid deficient" and is now called Down's Syndrome, although this wasn't apparent until he was about three months old. At first Mama and Papa told themselves that the baby was behind because of a bout with pneumonia he'd had at Christmas time. By spring, they had to face the truth, and for months they went from doctor to doctor while the baby boy remained barely alive.

The family doctor who first cared for Willie had been correct in his diagnosis, but under his treatment, the child became so much worse that he advised Mama and Papa to take the baby to a city doctor. The spring that Willie was eighteen months old they brought him home to die. They were out of money and deeply in debt. There were no dreams that year, just dull, heavy living from day to day. Because Papa had work to do in the field, he rigged up a flag for Mama to put on the windmill if she needed to call him home. He would make a round in the field and look to see if the flag was up, and then make another round, and so on through the day.

Papa was in town one day when he met the doctor who had first cared for Willie. As old friends, they stopped to talk. "How is the boy, Charley?"

Papa shook his head and said, "As bad as he can be and still live. Frankly, I don't see how he hangs on."

Doctor Wes hesitated and then said, "Charley, I'd like to try again to help your boy. I've been studying his case and I've been in touch with a doctor in the East. I still think Willie's problem is caused by a thyroid deficiency, but I wonder if I was giving him too much thyroid extract. I'd like to start him out again on smaller doses."

Papa said, "Well, I promised Ermie we wouldn't put him through any more torture, but I'll tell her what you've said to me. If she wants you to treat him, it's all right with me. Only, don't build up her hope as she's had about all she can take, and she's having another baby in the fall."

Doctor Wes was right and it was almost a miracle the way Willie responded. By his second birthday, Willie could sit alone and smiled and played like a baby six or eight months old.

Thus Mama and Papa were able to rejoice when a healthy baby girl was born. They named me Julia after Papa's mother. These were the family's early years—the years I can't remember.

Mama Never Liked Aunt Nelle

NO ONE EVER expected Papa's brother, Uncle Ed, to marry, not that he was so old, only twenty-seven. But girls always seemed to bore him and he liked to be alone most of the time. After Grandma died, he and Grandpa "batched" on what we called the Home Place. Grandpa did the cooking and chores and Uncle Ed did the farming.

Our family lived on a rented farm known as the Free Water Farm. It was seven miles from the Home Place, but despite the distance, Papa and Uncle Ed did a lot of work together.

Papa thought of Uncle Ed as his little brother and Mama had much the same idea. Maybe that's why she didn't think much of it when she saw the girl's picture in his watch.

It happened when we went up to the Home Place to thresh Uncle Ed's wheat. We all went as Mama had to cook for the threshing crew. We'd just finished threshing our own wheat, a job that lasted two weeks.

Papa and Uncle Ed had their own threshing rig. They threshed for about ten other farmers every year. They both loved any kind of machinery, but their special love was the steam engine and the threshing machine. Mama once said, "Charley, I do believe the reason you like to thresh so well is that the machine is always in need of repair, and you and Ed can spend so much time in your blacksmith shop."

I expected Papa to laugh but he answered seriously, "Well, sometimes blacksmithing can be mighty restful." I guess Mama understood because she didn't say any more.

Cooking for the threshers was a big job. Together with the family, there were ten or twelve at breakfast and eighteen or twenty for dinner at noon. Every meal was a banquet as Mama didn't take lightly her reputation of setting the best table in the county. Like all farm women, she baked her own bread, pies, and cakes, churned the butter, killed and dressed chickens, and gathered the vegetables from the garden for all the wonderful meals served to our help and neighbors at threshing time.

It was eight-thirty in the morning when we reached the Home Place to begin threshing. Papa went to the field at once to help set the rig. Setting the rig was rather complicated work. The tractor and separator had to be just a certain distance apart and perfectly in line before the big leather belt could connect them. Both machines had to be greased and oiled. The engine had to be fired up and a head of steam ready before the rest of the crew arrived right after dinner.

The permanent crew consisted of the engineer, who was Uncle Ed, and the separator man, who was Papa. In addition, a water boy hauled coal and water to the field, and usually some older man ran errands and was of general help.

The neighbors did the rest of the work, such as pitching the stacked wheat into the separator and hauling the threshed grain to the elevator in town, seven miles away. Since the hauling was done with horses, it was necessary to have a large crew. No wages were paid the neighbors as work was done in exchange when they threshed their own grain.

Mama brought bread and cake with her from her kitchen, and as she would only have nine or ten for dinner the first day, she was taking it rather easy. Then she noticed the clock had

stopped. Fearful that she wouldn't have dinner right on time, she sent me to the field to get Uncle Ed's watch. On the way back, I couldn't resist opening the case, and there in the lid was the picture of a very pretty girl. I could hardly wait to get to the house and ask Mama who the girl was in Uncle Ed's watch.

Taking the watch, Mama opened it to see what time it was and, without mentioning the picture, said, "My goodness, it's eleven o'clock. We'll have to hurry to get dinner on the table before the men come in."

She hung the watch by the chain on a nail and rushed to get the big kettle of potatoes on the stove. I knew this was no time to ask about the picture. "We'll have canned peas for a vegetable," Mama said as she opened three cans and put them in a pan on the back of the stove. She sent me to the cellar to get pickles, jelly and butter, then asked me to help set the table and run errands, all the while keeping an eye on Willie and our new baby, John.

We were all ready to dish up when Papa came in to get towels and soap so the men could wash before eating. The men preferred washing out by the well where they could use a big pail of water and splash as much as they pleased. A few minutes later they came in, washed and combed and joking about how hungry they were. This joking was a subtle compliment to the cook.

"How did you get along?" Mama asked of Papa as the men were getting seated.

"Fine," he answered. "We're all ready to roll. Ed is staying with the machine until I get back. He'll have to eat later on, so keep something warm for him."

"Sure," Mama answered, then asked, "How many will there be for supper?"

Papa thought for a minute before answering, "Probably about six more than for dinner. We won't have a full crew until tomorrow."

Mama kept busy passing food and filling bowls. I filled water glasses and bread plates and put on more cream and butter as it was needed.

As soon as the men had eaten, they hurried out to hitch up their teams, as the neighbors were already gathering for the afternoon work.

Papa stopped his team near the door and called out to Mama, "If you don't need Julia, she can sit in the tool box and watch us thresh this afternoon."

Heaven will never offer anything to equal the thrill of sitting in the tool box of a steam engine. It is terribly hot and you get chaff down your neck, but, oh, the excitement and the noise, and the tool box is a ringside seat. How I hoped Mama would say yes, but she hesitated before answering. "Yes, she can go, but let's have her wait and go out with Ed. She hasn't had any dinner yet and she can help me clear the table. Have her come in with the water boy about four o'clock as I'll need her to help with supper."

Joy of joys. I was not only going to sit in the tool box, but ride back on the water wagon, perched on a seat high up in front of the big steel water tank. At Mama's suggestion, I put on an old dark dress and my old slat sunbonnet, for I was sure to get some grease on my clothes.

Uncle Ed came in and ate his dinner and when we were about to leave, he asked Mama, "Ermie, do you need my watch any longer?"

"Why no," she said. "I started the clock and it seems to be running." Handing him his watch, she grinned and asked, "Are you going to tell us who the girl is in your watch?"

Uncle Ed blushed and said, "Oh, it's just a picture that was given to me as a joke. I don't even know who she is."

So it was that none of us thought any more about the girl in the watch case.

Threshing lasted for a week and everyone worked hard every day except Sunday. Even on Sunday, Mama had work to catch up on, while Papa and Uncle Ed made repairs on the engine and separator.

The night after we finished threshing Uncle Ed's wheat, supper seemed quiet after having had so many at the table. The conversation was mostly about wheat. Then Uncle Ed spoke up and said, "I'm going back East for a few days. I plan to take the train tomorrow morning. There won't be much to do now and Pa can do the chores."

Mama looked like she was going to say something and I thought of the girl in his watch, but it was Papa who spoke. "Good idea. You've been working hard all year and by this time next month, you will be too busy to get away."

We all assumed that Uncle Ed was going to Nebraska City or Lincoln to visit relatives and friends. Then Mama said, "Charley, why don't we stay here a few days, and I can do fall house cleaning for Pa and Ed? It will be easier than coming back later."

"Why yes," Papa answered. "Theodore's a dependable hired man, and I think he can take care of our place a few days longer. I'll be glad to have time to put the separator under cover for the winter."

The Home Place had a big old house and every spring and fall Mama cleaned it from top to bottom for Uncle Ed and Grandpa. After Uncle Ed left on his trip, Mama spent more than three days scrubbing floors, washing curtains and completing fall house cleaning. She even found time to do some baking in the morning before we left for home.

It took time to pack our clothes and get ready to leave so it was late in the afternoon before we reached home. Theodore had batched while we were gone. Theodore was no housekeeper. Dirty dishes were piled everywhere in the kitchen. A dust storm had deposited dust over everything. The screen door had blown open and millions of flies feasted on the dirty dishes. Somehow Mama got things cleaned up enough to give us supper and get us to bed. The rest would have to wait until morning.

But next morning Mama awoke with what we called one of "Mama's sick headaches." By tying a folded tea towel tightly around her head and clinging to the stove for support, she got breakfast on the table. Then waves of nausea and pain drove her back to bed. Helplessly, I followed her to the bedroom.

"Mama, can I get you some medicine or put a cold washcloth on your head?"

"No, dear," she said, "but if you will keep an eye on John and Willie and put the dishes in a pan to soak, I'll try to get up after a while."

I tried, but the day was gloomy and lonesome. Papa had to go to the field so the boys and I were alone. Mama got up at noon, long enough to wash a few dishes and fry some ham and potatoes. She looked so sick that I wondered how sick you had to be to die. She didn't get up again until about five o'clock that afternoon. She said she felt a little better and again washed a few dishes.

After combing and braiding my hair, she started a simple supper. I began to set the table when Mama said, "Set the table here in the kitchen. I don't feel like walking to the dining room and don't bother to put on a tablecloth. We'll eat just this once on the oilcloth."

We had just sat down to eat when we heard someone at the side door. Mama still had the towel on her head and her dress was rumpled from lying down. Papa went to answer the door which opened from the side porch into the kitchen. We heard him say, "Come in."

We looked up to see Uncle Ed and the girl in the watch case. Uncle Ed looked happier than I'd ever seen him and, turning his hand up in a rather silly gesture, said, "Meet the bride. Nelle, this is your new brother Charley and over here is Ermie."

Mama snatched the towel from her head before she got up to greet her new sister. "How nice," she said, "but why didn't you warn us we were having company?"

Uncle Ed answered, "We wanted to surprise you." Mama was smiling but I could see in her face all the thoughts about the dirty kitchen, the skimpy supper, the untidy children, and worst of all, eating on the oilcloth.

True to her nature, Mama made the best of the situation and, after we were all identified, she invited the guests into the living room. "Come Ed, take Nelle into the other room while I whip up a bite of supper."

Papa lit a lamp and led the way into the living room which was relatively neat. Mama turned and muttered, "Thunder and mud! Why didn't he phone us?"

We children and Theodore finished eating, then I went to the living room to get a better look at my new Aunt Nelle. She was sitting on Uncle Ed's lap and Papa was trying not to notice. Uncle Ed said, "Nelle wanted to go right out to my place but I wanted to surprise you and Ermie, so we hired a livery rig to bring us out here."

"This is my first trip this far west," said the new Aunt Nelle, "and Ed tried to tell me there were still Indians around."

Papa started to ask her where her home was when Mama came in and said, "I have some supper ready. Come to the dining room."

I guess the headache was gone as Mama had a white cloth on the dining table and a nice meal set out with places for four. She and Papa ate with the guests and while they were still talking about the wedding and Aunt Nelle's home in Wisconsin, Mama excused herself and went upstairs to convert my room into a guest chamber and to put a cot in the boys' room for me.

Mama must have worked hours after everyone was in bed because by the next morning the house was shining and breakfast was a feast.

After breakfast, when Papa brought the milk and cream into the kitchen, Mama stopped him to talk about the trip to take Uncle Ed and Aunt Nelle up to the Home Place. Then in a low tone she added, "Also, I think we should bring your father back with us. In fact, Charley, I think we should plan for him to come live with us."

Papa nodded and Mama went on, "He's been working too hard and now that Ed has Nelle to keep house, Pa can take it a little easier."

"I'll ask him," Papa said, and then with a grin, he turned to Mama and added, "What will you bet she can't cook?"

Papa hitched the best team of trotters to the carriage and, at ten o'clock, we set out for Uncle Ed's house. I don't remember much of what was said during the ride except Aunt Nelle kept talking about going to "Bachelors' Hall." Uncle Ed told her not to expect too much.

Papa stopped the team near the front door and we all got out. Grandpa came up from the barn. Papa went to meet him and explained the situation before taking him around to meet Aunt Nelle.

Uncle Ed took his bride by the arm and led her into the house. With a wide spread of his arms, he said, "Welcome to Bachelors' Hall."

Looking wide-eyed, she answered, "How cute and how nice and clean. I think I married a wonderful housekeeper."

"Not bad, huh?" said Uncle Ed, with never a word of how Mama had scoured Bachelors' Hall, and I knew Mama would never like Aunt Nelle, nor forgive Uncle Ed.

The Big Room

OUR HOUSE AT our new place in southern Nebraska, Free Water Farm, was a white, two-story Victorian with three covered porches. The parlor had an oak floor, ornate oak trim around the doors and windows, and the walls were covered with a deep red wallpaper, embellished with huge gilded scrolls and medallions of roses. The gild was so heavy that when I scraped it, I collected a little pile of gold dust on my thumbnail. The parlor was eighteen by thirty feet and had a bay window on the end facing the road. It was a room that called out for a grand piano, Oriental rugs and French furniture, none of which we had. As a result, it was never furnished. The dining room was large enough to double as a living room.

The Room was not without purpose. In July and August, when it was unbearably hot upstairs, Mama brought our family beds down and lined them up in this large room where it was reasonably cool. In the winter, when it was too cold and the snow was too deep to play outside, we children put our coats and caps on and ran up and down the Room, pulling our wagons and carts. Also, Mama used the Room to dry her laundry. I guess she figured that if Dolly Madison could hang her wash in the Green Room, she could hang hers in the Red Room.

After we became acquainted with our neighbors at the farm near Wilcox, they told us that the former occupants held dances in the Red Room, and they wondered if we could continue the custom. They went on to say that my parents wouldn't have to furnish anything except the Room and the ice to make ice cream. They would bring the ice cream ingredients and cake. They would also pay the musicians and help clean up afterward. They said that it would be by invitation only, just couples, and there would be no drinking. It sounded like fun to my mother and father, so they agreed to carry on the tradition.

The first dance was on a Saturday night in mid-September. Mama cleaned the whole house, including the Room, served an early supper and put the boys to bed upstairs. After she dressed herself, she helped me into a dotted swiss dress and tied French blue ribbons in my hair. She said nothing about me going to bed early. For some reason, my mother always allowed me to set my own bed time and Papa often said, "Julia never goes to bed until the last dog's hung," whatever that meant.

A little before seven o'clock, wagons and carriages began to arrive, and the men brought three big twelve-quart ice cream freezers into the kitchen along with cakes and extra dishes which were set on the table. The men brought in a big two-by-sixteen inch plank, placed it on wooden boxes down the long side of the Big Room, and covered it with lap robes to furnish a seating area. Two people took blocks of paraffin and a sharp knife and walked around shaving the paraffin onto the dance floor. They took up a collection to pay the musicians. It must have cost about twenty-five cents a person because there were between thirty and forty people there. The musicians were paid $7.50 for the evening or $2.50 each. At seven o'clock, the musicians arrived and took their place in the bay window. One played a violin, another an accordion, and I can't remember what the third musician played. Shortly, they started the dance. It was customary for the men to dance with their wife or girlfriend for the first dance, the supper dance, and the last dance of the night. But since Papa couldn't dance, Mama sat out these three dances. However, she was on the floor by the second dance and was evidently enjoying it very much. I stood watching her and I thought she was the prettiest person on the floor. During the supper dance, two or three couples went to the kitchen, uncovered the ice cream, sliced the cake and got ready for the supper. People came rushing out to get their cake and ice cream and a cup of coffee. Some of them sat around the dining room table and ate. Some went out on the porch and others just stood around the kitchen or the Big Room and ate. In about a half hour, everyone was ready to dance again. After the supper dance, it seemed that the music was more lively. People seemed ready to have a good time.

At twelve o'clock, they played "Good Night Ladies" and then, there was a mad scramble to get to the kitchen, clean up, and get ready to go home. They washed dishes, carried out ice cream freezers, and packed up dishes they had brought. The big plank was taken out and, in thirty minutes, everybody was gone. It seemed that everyone had a good time, including my parents.

Our October dance was much like the September one, except the morning after the dance, Papa complained that they had left some work for Mama to do. They left the kitchen slightly messy, and he didn't think it was right after they had said they would take care of everything.

They called the dance held in November the Harvest Dance, and everybody thought that it was special. It was to be the last dance of the season and everybody came much more dressed up. Mama had a black taffeta skirt with a fourteen-inch flounce on the bottom and a pale blue cashmere wool blouse. She really did look pretty. Everybody danced and had such a good time. Three or four dances after the supper dance, the violinist, who also liked to dance, asked one of the women who could handle a bow to relieve him so he could have a couple of dances. He had his first dance with his sister-in-law who was a very good dancer. For the next dance, he asked Mama. He leaned over and said something to the musicians and when they started playing, it was a very fast, lively tune. Some of the couples gave up and walked to the side of the floor and just watched. For some reason, Mama's partner let loose of her, stepped back two paces, bowed to her and went into a jig. Mama looked surprised, but not to be undone, she spread her skirts and went into a jig also. When the music ended, the man bowed to her, left her standing in the middle of the floor, and went back over to pick up his fiddle. Mama walked over to where Papa and I were watching.

Papa grinned and said, "I didn't know you could do that."

People were laughing and clapping and she was a little embarrassed. "Oh, I haven't done that for years, not since I left Ohio. My brother taught me and we used to do it all the time."

Our neighbor, Newt, came to ask her for the next dance and she said, "Thank you, but I have to catch my breath." So she stood there with Papa and me throughout that dance and then was back on the floor and danced the rest of the evening. Shortly after the music stopped, everybody said goodnight and was gone.

The next morning when I came downstairs, I heard Papa talking in an agitated manner, "I don't care, Erma, I'm going to tell them. No more dances."

"Oh Charley, don't say anything. I don't want any trouble in the neighborhood. It's the last dance of the year. Next time they want to dance, we'll just tell them we're too busy." Mama said.

The next year Mama was pregnant with the twins and so nobody mentioned having a dance. The year after that, for some reason, it just didn't come up, and there were never any more dances in the Big Room. And so it was that Mama never had another chance to dance. She was never on a dance floor again.

The Wonderful Blackboard

M Y PARENTS ORDERED the blackboard for my fourth birthday in 1906. Uncle Ed brought it out from town that afternoon and set it up. Its writing surface was about two by two feet, with a chalk tray below that, and up above was a paper roller printed with things that you could copy or write. The roller had the alphabet in capital and lower case letters in print and in script, as well as simple pictures of flowers, fruit and animals and one group of dimensional drawings, such as boxes and houses. After Uncle Ed had the blackboard set up, he turned the roller to the alphabet and pointed to the letter C and said, "This is a C, this is an A, and this is an N." He wrote them on the board and said, "Now that is 'can.' You learn your letters and then you can learn to read."

Learn to read? I had no idea that children could learn to read. I knew adults could read. In fact, they read to me almost every day, but I thought only they knew how to do it. I had no idea that I could ever learn. I told him so and he pointed out and pronounced each letter in the alphabet, and then, picking up a newspaper, he ran his finger down a column until he came to the word "can" and showed it to me. He said, "See here? That's 'can.'" He read the sentence to me and said, "Every time you come to that word, you say 'can.'"

I was never so excited in my life. He told me to try it. I

managed in some fashion to write "can" and Uncle Ed left shortly afterward. I spent the rest of the afternoon writing "can" on
the blackboard and finding the word in newspapers. Each time
I'd carry it to my mother and sometimes I would find the word
"can" in another word such as can't or candle. She explained to
me that just part of the word was "can," and I'd have to learn
other words like "candle" and "can't." After she got tired enough
of the word "can," she wrote "boy" and "girl" and "baby" on the
blackboard. I tried to write them and I tried to find them on the
roller. This kept me quite busy. The next afternoon when I got
ready to write, she said, "Would you like to write your name?"
And so she printed my name, but she used the large J and
explained to me that the big letters, as she called them, were
always used to begin a name. So I contented myself with writing
my name and those three words.

Day by day, I learned more and more words. I looked for
words in my story books and copied them on the blackboard.
My birthday was in November, and, by Christmas, I was reading
well enough to read my Mother Goose book that I got for
Christmas that year.

Uncle Ed was impressed with what I was writing and told
me, "You go ahead and learn your letters better and learn to
write these words and when you're five, you can go to school."

I'd heard of school but I had no idea what it was. Willie
didn't go to school and John was too little to go to school, and I
didn't play with any children who went to school. Uncle Ed
explained as best he could what school was and told me I would
learn many words. He also helped me learn the numbers and I
copied them off the roller.

It was great fun. I worked at it all winter and could hardly
wait until summer was over and fall came and I could go to
school. Unfortunately, when fall came my mother was pregnant,

unable to take me to school, and I was too young and too small to go the mile and a half all alone. So she told me I'd have to wait until the next year. I was broken-hearted but she said, "Well, sometimes we just can't help these things. I'll buy you books, and you can study all you want at home."

The next time she went to town, she got me a First Reader and I learned to read and copy the words from it. Then she got me story books and while Mama was busy with the new twins Rita and Raymond, I was reading. It wasn't too bad to wait another year till I was six.

When I went to school the next September, the teacher handed me a book and started to teach me.

"I can read that," I said and started reading.

"Oh, can you read?"

I said, "Yes," as if to say, why shouldn't I read? So instead of putting me in the primary class, she put me in the first grade. I went to school a whole month, but a diphtheria epidemic broke out and my mother took me out of school. With twin babies and my two brothers, she couldn't risk having me bring any disease home from school. She said when the diphtheria scare was over, I could go back to school. But it was followed by scarlet fever and measles, then mumps, and each time, I was told I couldn't go to school until there was no more disease in the neighborhood. It wasn't until the next May that I was able to return to school.

In the meantime, Mama bought books and helped me with numbers. When I went back to school, the teacher put me in second grade and because of all the training I'd had, I was able to hold my own in the class. When May 30 came and school was out, I was passed into the third grade. Nobody thought it was odd that I'd only gone to school two months and was promoted to the third grade. Country school was very flexible.

The next year I was in third grade and I got bored with arithmetic. There weren't enough arithmetic books for the whole class so the teacher put the problems on the blackboard in front of the schoolroom, and the youngsters worked from that. I worked all the problems for my grade and then did the problems for the fourth grade. I remember one time the fourth graders were doing long division. At that time, children learned to do long division by having a left angle and putting the divisor in that. The dividend was in the middle and a right angle was on the right-hand side of the numbers for the quotient. That was also the way I drew a girl. I would always draw the neck and shoulders, round out the head, then draw arms and body. I went home and said to my mother, "Could you show me how to do the kind of arithmetic that you put the numbers on a girl's neck?"

She said, "What do you mean, put numbers on a girl's neck?"

I showed her and she said, "Oh, that's long division. You don't want to do that, do you?"

I said, "Yes, I do," and I showed her I'd copied down the problems and brought them home. So she showed me how to do long division. I worked all the problems and the next morning I took them to school and presented them to the teacher but she got real cross with me. She said, "You have no business working fourth grade arithmetic. You should just work the third grade problems."

So for the rest of the year, I worked the fourth grade arithmetic and took it home for my mother to correct, not letting the teacher know.

In country school, the classes recited in the front of the classroom. I held a book up in front of me and pretended to study. I was very curious and I listened, whether it was fourth, fifth, sixth or seventh grade, history, geography, or physiology.

Then I went home and asked my mother questions. So I really studied several grades at once. Later on this proved to be a great deal of help to me because I had to miss a lot of school.

We had no libraries and there were a limited number of children's books sold in town. The drugstore carried a few and my mother bought these for me. I soon began reading adult magazines and books, which I never would have done without this chance to listen to other classes. But it all started with my little blackboard. In fact, the blackboard was the beginning of my entire education.

Those Foreigners

I WAS THRILLED WHEN I learned how Free Water Farm got its name. When this part of southern Nebraska had been homesteaded, water was scarce and precious. The water veins ran deep, far too deep for a well to be dug by hand. To drill two hundred feet, buy pipe and casing, plus a pump and windmill, was beyond the means of most homesteaders. Those who did drill a well felt that they couldn't afford to give away water, so they sold it by the barrel. But when Heinrick Van Syke homesteaded the land we later lived on, he drilled a two-inch well and dredged out quite a large pond. He let his windmill run day and night and the water overflowed from his cattle tank into the pond. He then announced that the water was free.

People came for miles with wagons and barrels. The place became known as Free Water Farm. In time there was Free Water Church, Free Water School and even Free Water Precinct.

Free Water Farm was a lovely place. Big trees grew around the house and pond. An ice house stood by the pond, and every winter Papa cut ice and packed it in straw for the next summer. Mr. Van Syke had built fine barns and a large friendly house.

What we didn't find at Free Water Farm was neighbors. On one side of us was an old lagoon that was swampy in the spring and dry and cracked in the summer. On the other side were several families of foreigners, German immigrants who neither wanted

us nor needed us. Both Mama and Papa tried to be neighborly to the Germans. We once went to their church, but since the sermon was in German and no one spoke to us, we didn't go again.

It was the custom for farmers to band together in crews and thresh each man's crop in turn. Papa had gone to Herman Groate and Oscar Heidel, the two nearest German neighbors, to exchange threshing work but they said they had a full crew, so Papa had to go six miles to join another crew.

I had an unhappy experience with the Groate children. My brothers, John, Willie and I took our wagon down the road to pick up black walnuts. The Groate children were there also picking up walnuts. The trees were on our land but Mama said there was enough for all. They yelled something at us in German. Willie, who had a speech impediment, said something to them and they mimicked him. I protested and they threw dirt on us. We went home and decided we didn't like foreigners, Germans in particular except Theodore Lingenfelder, a young German immigrant Papa had previously hired to help on the farm. Of course he lived with us like one of the family. Theodore was kind, patient and hard-working. We soon learned that we could like a foreigner. We all helped him learn English and he taught us some German words. Our lessons were usually at the table so we learned to say brod for bread, bodder for butter and sooner for spoon.

That summer Papa tried again to be neighborly with the Germans as Theodore could speak the language and had made a few friends among them.

In the fall of our second year at Free Water Farm, Mr. Groate finally came to us as a neighbor. I remember it was about one o'clock when I saw him walk into our yard. He was a short, powerfully-built man, with reddish hair and a fair mustache. Like all farmers, he wore bib overalls, but was wearing a home-knit sweater which was longer than the old suit coat he wore over it. He carried a walking stick made from a branch with a gnarled joint forming the handle. Hanging over his shoulder by a leather strap was a cog wheel from a piece of machinery.

Papa answered his knock with, "Good afternoon, Mr. Groate, won't you come in?"

Mr. Groate replied, "Good afternoon, Sharley. No I won't come in, I have this greasy wheel," and he took it off his shoulder. "I hear by Theodore you are good blacksmith and have a forge, so I think maybe you can fix this."

Papa stepped out onto the porch and, looking at the wheel, asked, "What seems to be the trouble?"

Mr. Groate explained, "It is from my manure spreader. I have had it so long I can not get parts and the wheel slips all the time."

"Oh yes," Papa said, "you need to have a sleeve fitted in to take up the slack. I can do that. Just wait until I get my jacket and we'll go down to the shop."

I followed, as I seldom missed a chance to watch Papa work in the shop. Papa'd been working that morning and there was still a fire in the forge. A few puffs with the big bellows and it was hot again. I don't know exactly what Papa did but by three o'clock the wheel was repaired, and I could see the men becoming friends.

Ordinarily we didn't have an afternoon lunch, but Mama knew it was a German custom so she sent little John down to say lunch was ready. Mr. Groate protested that he didn't want to be a bother and wasn't dressed to go in our house. But Papa said, "Mr. Groate, you are my neighbor and you must eat with us."

We went to the house and after Mr. Groate was introduced to Mama and Grandpa, we sat down at the kitchen table to have fresh cinnamon rolls and coffee. Coffee for us children was milk served in a coffee cup. Mama asked Mr. Groate how many children he had and he answered, "Well, now we have twelve but in two months we have thirteen. Maybe that is unlucky."

I wondered how he knew they would have another, then I remembered hearing someone say that Germans had a baby every other year. I knew little Ernest Groate was almost two, so this must be the year for them to have a baby. We children left the table but Papa, Mama and Mr. Groate sat and talked for a long time. Mama made another pot of coffee. I heard Mama say, "We hope you and Mrs. Groate will come visit us some time soon."

Mr. Groate stammered, "We did not think we were fine enough to come see you. You talk too nice, and you had feather in your hat when you came to our church. You did not come again, and we thought you did not like us." Mama laughed and that seemed to relax everyone.

Mr. Groate got up from the table saying, "I must go now, I want to drive my cows home. My bull is very mean and I wouldn't want my children to go to the pasture."

Papa looked at him seriously and said, "I have heard of your bull, and I would think you would be afraid of him yourself."

Mr. Groate held up his cane by the small end and brandished the knot, gave a knowing look, and said, "With this I am not afraid. The bull, he knows who is boss."

"Well, I'm afraid of an animal like that and I wouldn't want to meet him with just a stick." Papa said.

Mr. Groate laughed, "Don't worry, Sharley, next week he is going to market." With that he left and Papa went to the barn to help Theodore with the chores.

Mama was getting supper and I was setting the table when I turned to ask her, "Why does Mr. Groate call Papa 'Sharley'"?

"Well, Sister," she said, "it's because he learned to speak German before English. It's like when you asked Theodore how to say girl in German and when you tried to say the word, it came out 'may chin.' You tried again and again but you couldn't say it like Theodore did."

We were just finishing supper that evening when the phone rang. Mama got up and answered, then turned to Papa. "Charley, it's for you. It's Mr. Heidel and he sounds so strange."

Papa went to the phone, "Hello, Oscar." He listened then said, "No, he was here but he left a couple of hours ago, said he was going to drive his cows home." Papa looked frightened when he said, "He's probably all right, but I'll get my lantern and come right up." Turning from the phone, Papa told us, "Herman Groate didn't get home. His cattle came home and the bull was excited and bellowed when anyone came near the barnyard. They're getting up a search party."

Just then the general alarm sounded on the phone. Neighbors cranked out seven or eight long rings on the wall phones to alert people to an emergency. Mama picked up the receiver, listened a moment and hung up. "It's a general call for help," she said.

Papa checked to see if there was plenty of oil in the lantern. He lit the wick, lowered the flue and set the lantern on the table while he put on his coat. Then he went over and kissed Mama and said, "Pray it isn't too bad."

Mama nodded, went to the window and said, "Look, you can see the lanterns in the Groate pasture."

Papa went out the door but before he was off the porch, Mama was calling, "Charley, where's the bull now?"

Papa turned, "Oscar Heidel said the bull went in the barn and the Groate kids locked him in."

For two hours we watched the lanterns go back and forth across the pasture. Mama put the boys to bed but didn't clear the table. It was the first time I'd ever known her to let the table stand. She was quiet except to say it was too bad we didn't go back to the German church again. As we watched, the lanterns of two or three men stopped and one man waved a lantern over his head. Then lanterns from all over the pasture began to gather in one spot.

Grandpa, who had been watching from the dining room window, came to the kitchen and, looking at Mama, said, "That doesn't look good to me."

Mama shook her head sadly and replied, "I'm afraid of what they found, Pa." Turning to me, she said, "Don't you think you should go to bed, Julia? Papa won't be home for a long time."

I was tired but asked, "Will you call me when Papa comes home? I'm worried, too."

"I'll call you," she said, "but Papa may bring very bad news."

I got ready for bed knowing Mama would call me. She always treated me like an adult and respected my wishes if I was well-behaved. I took off my shoes and put them behind the stove before going upstairs, then turned to Mama and said, "I'm glad Mr. Groate had lunch with us."

"So am I, dear," she replied. "Very glad indeed."

I slept fitfully until Mama called me at midnight. "Papa's coming. I can see his lantern coming down the road. I promised to call you but you can go back to sleep if you want to, and I'll tell you about it in the morning."

"No," I answered. "I want to get up. When I came downstairs, Mama was putting coffee on and I knew she and Grandpa had been waiting all the time. Papa came in the door, his face grey and sad.

"Is he…? Is he…?" Mama couldn't say the word.

Papa answered, "Yes, he's dead." He blew out the lantern and sat down before saying any more. "It was awful. The man never had a chance."

Mama poured him some coffee, and he drank it so hot I knew it burned his mouth. Then he said, "I had to go tell Mrs. Groate. It was the hardest thing I have ever been asked to do."

"Why? Why you?" Mama asked. "When all their friends and relatives were there?"

"Well," Papa said, "they insisted that I would know better how to tell her. The truth was, no one needed to tell her. She knew by the look of our faces what we had to say. The German preacher was there and was a big help."

"Did you go back for the body?" Mama asked.

"No," Papa answered. "The preacher asked me to stay for a while. The men took a binder canvas and a wagon and went out to the pasture. They won't be able to show the body. Oscar Heidel is too broken up to do anything. But Otis Rosier and Ernest Metz are working now to lay him out. As soon as I rest a little, I'll go to the ice house and get some ice to take up. They'll need it."

Our family was a long time forgetting the tragedy of the Groate family. During the next four or five weeks, Mrs. Groate asked several times for my mother to come spend time with her and advise her. Then one evening about eight o'clock, Carl, the oldest Groate boy, came and asked Mama to come at once.

Mama got ready to leave, then looked to me, saying "Sister, Mrs. Groate needs me very badly. I want you to put the children to bed, then you go to bed. I think I'll be back in time to get breakfast, but if I'm not, you help Papa and Grandpa and be an especially good girl." I promised and she left hurriedly.

Grandpa and I were getting breakfast the next morning when Mama came home. She looked tired but happy. Looking about, she said, "My, what a nice breakfast we're having, and I have good news. Mrs. Groate has a lovely new baby boy."

Papa came in just then with a pail of fresh milk and grinning at Mama, said, "A boy, huh?"

"Yes," Mama said, "an eight-pound boy, and I think we have made friends with our neighbors at last."

"What's his name?" I interrupted.

Mama looked at Papa when she answered, "His name is Sharley Adolph Groate."

Justice

I N 1908, ALMOST every little girl had a playhouse, and why not? We expected to grow up to be housewives, and this was one way of pretending that we were already grown. I loved building a playhouse. I would assemble my chipped dishes, leaky pans, boxes and so forth and arrange them in an orange-crate cupboard. Somehow my interest lagged after the playhouse was arranged and I'd become discontent. I moved often. I had a playhouse on the end of the back porch, one in the granary, another under the apple tree, and finally, a playhouse in an empty space of the haymow.

I had decided to make mud pies in my haymow playhouse and was carrying a can of water and another can of dry dirt. I climbed up the ladder from the feed space in the barn into the haymow. When I got into the haymow, I saw a man lying on the hay. I recognized him; it was Mike. Mike was the water boy or errand boy who worked for Papa and Uncle Ed. They were out in the field planting wheat, using the big Case steam tractor pulling three six-foot drills behind it. Mike's job was to haul coal out to fuel the tractor and to drive the horse-drawn water tank, getting water from the windmill, and hauling it to the tractor. He also took the seed-wheat to the field or did anything else that was needed to help keep the rig going.

I asked, "Why aren't you out in the field?"

"Oh, I got sick and your uncle told me to come in and lie down on the hay until he could take me home."

I was so surprised to have someone in the haymow that I didn't pay any attention to where I was going. I stumbled and fell down but managed not to spill my cans. I climbed up and Mike said, "Do that again."

"Do what again?" I asked.

"Fall down."

Believing I'd done some very comical, circus-like act, I promptly made an elaborate fall onto the hay, and then he said to me, "Now unbutton your panties."

"What?" I said.

"Unbutton your panties."

I jumped up, ran over to and down the ladder, across the yard, into the house as fast as I could go. Mama had her back turned to me and was working at the cook stove. She didn't pay any attention to me. I wanted to tell her what happened but I didn't know how to begin. I fidgeted around the kitchen from chair to chair. Finally I blurted out, "I don't think Mike will go to heaven when he dies."

"Why?" Mama asked, looking at me strangely.

"Because he talks bad."

"What do you mean he talks bad?"

I had my opening and I told her what happened. She took me by the shoulders and said, "Did he touch you?"

I said, "No."

"Did he touch your panties?"

"No."

"Are you sure he didn't touch your panties?"

"No, he didn't have a chance. I ran down the ladder and came to the house."

She said, "You did exactly right and I'm very proud of you.

He's a very bad man. I don't want you to ever go near him again. In fact, don't ever go into the barn again when there're any men there unless Papa or Uncle Ed are with you."

"But Mama, I didn't know he was there. I thought he was out in the field."

"I know you did and you did exactly right." Then with her usual cure-all she said, "Would you like a piece of bread with butter and sugar?"

While I was eating my bread and butter and sugar, she stepped out the door and came back a few minutes later and set something down on the porch. Then she got out a pan of potatoes and sat down to peel them, but situated herself where she could look out the back door. A few minutes later she set the pan down, jumped up and said, "You stay here."

She ran out the back door and picked up a horse whip, which she evidently had left there a few minutes earlier. I looked and saw Mike coming out of the barn. Mama ran toward him. He saw her coming and tried to dodge, but she was too quick for him. She lashed him across the back and shoulders with the whip. He ran down the long driveway toward the road with her behind him, whipping him with every step. When he got to the road, he turned left toward town. She followed him an eighth of a mile, beating him unmercifully. His back must have been a mass of welts and blood because a whip applied harshly can raise a welt on the skin of a horse. It's not hard to imagine what it could do to a man.

She came back to the house and didn't say a word. Neither did I, for some reason. A little later, Papa and Uncle Ed came in from the field and Mama went out to meet them. I waited a minute or two and then slowly followed. I knew she was telling them what had happened and, as I drew near, I heard Papa say, "It's a good thing I wasn't here; I'd a-killed him."

And then Uncle Ed looked at Mama and said, "Ermie, you're a wonder. Imagine a woman being able to do that. It took a lot of courage. Next to tar and feathers, the worst thing that can happen to a man is to be horse-whipped, let alone by a woman."

As I came nearer, they changed the subject and I never heard it mentioned again. I forgot all about it until after I was grown and something brought it to my mind one day so I asked my mother, "Mama, do you remember the time you horse-whipped Mike?"

She said, "Yes, do you remember that? I didn't think you did."

"I forgot about it until recently. It just came back to me. What happened after that?"

She said, "Well, the next day your father went to see the sheriff to swear out a warrant for Mike's arrest. The sheriff said to him, 'Charley, I'll do it if you want me to, but I advise against it. The story'll get out all over the country and first thing you know, they'll say that your little girl was really harmed and then they'll say things about your wife. I'll tell you what I'd like to do, since your wife has already given him more punishment than the court would. I'll go see him. I won't go to his house because, although he comes from a worthless family, I don't want to hurt his mother. I'll tell him that you're going to swear out a warrant for his arrest, and I'll advise him to leave town and never come back.'"

And then Mama added, "I guess that's what happened because a few days later, Mike was gone, and as far as I know, he never returned."

The End of a Perfect Day

MAMA WAS GETTING supper in the kitchen. She sang softly. I heard the crackle of the corncob fire and the sizzle of the home-cured ham that was frying. The kitchen was full of good smells—the smoke from the ham, the fresh bread cooling beneath a white dish towel.

It was a delightful time of day and, after setting the table, I fitted myself into the niche between the hot water reservoir and the wall to watch, listen, and smell. It was then I heard the words Mama was singing, "At the End of a Perfect Day."

I pondered a moment before asking, "What's a perfect day, Mama?"

She laughed and said, "Well," and paused there to put more cobs on the fire. I knew I'd have to wait for an answer. She continued, "I guess it's when nothing happens from morning until night to make you sad or mean or unhappy. And it should have two very nice things happen, one to make the morning perfect and another for the afternoon."

I thought for a while and then said, "There aren't very many 'end-of-a-perfect days' are there?"

"No," Mama answered, "but there are quite a lot of 'end-of-an-almost-perfect days.'"

"Have you ever had a day that was clear, clear, clear perfect, Mama?" I asked.

Again, I had to wait while she filled the stove and turned the ham. I wondered if the perfect day was the time she wore the grey taffeta dress with the violet ribbon ruching at the neck. I knew she kept that dress because of some happy memory.

Then I got my answer, "Yes, I've had my share of perfect days."

"Tell me one," I begged. "Tell me why it was perfect."

She smiled and said, "Well, the most recent was the time Papa and I drove the colts to Lincoln, but it's too near supper time now to tell you about that day."

I decided to save that story for sometime when we were tearing carpet rags or Mama was churning. Both were good times for talking.

I started watching for my own "end-of-a-perfect day." Several times I almost had one, but each was marred in some way. Once, a wonderful day was spoiled because I had to say I was sorry for something I didn't think was my fault. Another day started out beautifully. Mama had made a blue chambray dress for my doll in the morning and showed me how to whip lace on the tiny ruffles. In the afternoon, she let me help her make sugar cookies. This is it, I thought. This will be a perfect day. But I reckoned without knowing how many warm cookies I had eaten, and before the day was over, I was a sick little girl. It wasn't the retching stomach that made me cry, it was the disappointment that I'd spoiled a perfect day.

"Hear, hear," Mama said, "you don't cry over a mere tummy ache that you yourself caused. Really, it's your tummy that should be sad."

When I explained my tears, she said, "That's what I meant about almost perfect days, and because we have so many of them, we don't cry because they aren't absolutely perfect. In fact," she added, "perfect days usually come when we least expect them."

So it was with my perfect day. It was a day early in November. I had awakened early and slipped quietly downstairs. No one was about but a fire burned in the kitchen stove so I knew Mama had started it and crawled back into bed for a nap while the kitchen warmed up. I was only six and too young to start a fire but I was allowed to put cobs in through the side door of the fire box. The fire was low, but a few minutes later I heard it crackle. I washed my hands at the kitchen sink and set the table. I was trying to think of something I could cook to surprise Mama when she came into the kitchen.

She acted surprised and said, "Don't tell me the brownies are getting breakfast."

We both laughed, then she said, "With such a good hot oven, we'll have biscuits and open the first jar of grape jelly." She started getting out the flour and lard and I noticed she had her pretty, early-in-the-morning look and was moving quickly, almost on her toes.

Mama's biscuits were a delight and with them went sausage cakes and "poog-grease," a gravy made with water and fryings.

John and Willie, or Boo, as we called him, awoke and I helped them dress, while Mama took care of the twins. Later, Papa told me, "Julia, I'm going to snap some corn. Do you want to ride along?"

"Oh yes, but I have to tell Mama." I ran to the house to tell her, then ran back and climbed up into the wagon. Papa let me ride in the front of the wagon because he was only going to be in the field an hour or two. When he stayed out all morning, I got too tired.

What fun to ride and pretend I was driving. The horses knew to move and keep just so far in front of the picker and never needed to be told when to move ahead. It was exciting to have the big ears of corn hit the bang board just above and behind my head. Later, the corn started sliding down around my feet and I chose two nice ears to use for making corncob dolls. When we came in with our "jag" of corn, Papa unhitched and left the wagon in the hog yard where the corn would be scooped off for feed. I was allowed to drive the unhitched team over to the buggy where Papa again fastened the neck yoke, tugs, and other straps.

We drove up to the house and Papa called out to Mama, "Ermie, I'm going down to Rosiers to borrow a wire stretcher. Is it all right for Julia to go along?"

"Yes," Mama answered, "if her face is clean. Why not take John and Willie, too, so I can get my ironing finished?"

Mama put coats and caps on the boys and brought them out to the buggy. Then, as she was more particular than Papa about faces, we had to wait while she went back for a wet washcloth and went over my face and pushed loose hair back under my cap.

The Rosiers lived a mile down the road and it was a pleasant ride. We didn't stay long. Papa got the stretcher and said a few words to Oat Rosier. Mrs. Rosier gave us some oatmeal cookies. On the way home John went to sleep.

By the time we got back, Mama had dinner ready. All that I remember having was cornbread. Mama had too much batter and baked the extra in a small pie pan which we called Johnnie Cake. I cut it into three pieces and gave the largest to John because it was, after all, Johnnie Cake.

After dinner, I decided to make my corncob dolls, and, wanting a warm place to work, I thought of the straw stack in the calf pen. Carefully I gathered my supplies. Into a large paper sack went the two ears of corn, several small pieces of cloth, my scissors, colors, and some lengths of ribbon. Also added was my Mother Goose book and cookies, crackers, an apple, and some raisins for a lunch. I put on my wraps, told Mama where I was going, and set out with my sack and a tomato can of water to be used on the dolls' hair.

Up the sloping side of the straw stack I climbed and then down into a depression on the sunny side of the stack. If you have never been in the depression of a straw stack after the wind has blown away the beards, you can't know what a wonderful place it is. The wind is shut off, the sun shines in, and you have perfect privacy, a safe distance from home.

To make corncob dolls, you peel back the husks one at a time, very carefully so as not to break them. Then you slowly shell the corn, saving the kernels to feed the chickens or pigs later. Next you soak the husks in water so they can be shredded and become doll's hair. While soaking the heads, it is well to have some good reading matter such as *Mother Goose Tales*.

I became so engrossed in my book and the sun was so warm, I could scarcely stir myself to finish my dolls. An apple and some crackers revived me, and I found the heads just right to finish. With a hairpin, I slit each husk several times, turned them back, and made two tight braids. On the ends, I tied tiny bows of ribbon. With the points of my red and blue crayons I made dots for eyes and a mouth. Wrapping a piece of cloth about their bodies, I tied sashes just beneath their chins. My dolls were completed. I had several real dolls, but always enjoyed corncob dolls. Mama told me that many children she knew as a child had only corncob dolls because their parents couldn't afford fifteen cents for a store doll.

The sun was low and my nest was getting cool. I gathered up my sack and dolls to take to the house to show Mama. "Look, Mama, see my dolls."

"What pretty dolls. I think they are the nicest I've ever seen. I'm glad you're back. It's getting cold, and I want you to play with the boys while I get supper." We played cross bull, a game played on all fours. The bull chases the other players under chairs and tables.

Supper was beef hash and chocolate pudding. Papa told Mama that Oat Rosier was going to vote for Teddy Roosevelt. Papa couldn't understand why, being a Bryan supporter himself. I couldn't understand all of it but I loved to hear Papa talk.

After supper, Mama allowed me to dry the silver. I helped her get the boys into bed. Then Mama read me a chapter from *Our Cousins of Many Lands.*

It was my bedtime and as I climbed in, I thought of my day. It had been perfect.

"Mama, Mama," I called out. "It was just as you said. I had a perfect day without knowing it. Today was clear, clear perfect."

"Yes," she said, "you've had a wonderful day."

"Will you sing it, Mama?" I asked.

As she started to sing, I nestled down into bed to savor my "End of a Perfect Day," which ended in sleep before she finished the song.

Gypsies

GYPSY CARAVANS WEREN'T an unusual sight on our southern Nebraska roads in the early 1900s. During the summer, at least two caravans would pass our farmhouse. There were usually eight to ten vehicles drawn by small, thin ponies. The ponies seemed strong, but looked undernourished. The first vehicle was an open wagon containing water barrels and some hay and grain for the ponies, while the second wagon carried tents, tent poles and big kettles.

In addition to the driver, two or three men and a few teenaged boys rode in each of the open wagons. Following them were the regular gypsy wagons and the box wagons with canvas tops stretched over hoops, a little like what we called covered wagons, except that the canvas was brightly colored, painted with flowers and symbols. The wheels of all the vehicles were bright yellow. An open carriage and maybe a top-buggy followed the covered wagons. They too were painted with emblems and flowers. Small dogs trotted along between the wheels under the wagons.

Extra horses were tied behind the rigs. Sometimes older boys or young men rode bareback alongside the caravan or up ahead of it. The men wore tight pants and bright shirts. They had leather hatbands adorned with coins and baubles around broad-brimmed, black felt hats.

The driver of the first wagon always seemed to be the leader of the gypsy band. Quite often, they'd stop in front of the house, and the leader would come in to ask my father if they could water their horses.

Papa said, "No, not at the tank. You can have all the water you want if you water them out of a bucket, but they can't drink out of the tank." My father was very particular about his horses; he always guarded against someone's stock spreading a disease to our horses.

The gypsies took some buckets, watered all their ponies and filled their water barrels. While they did this, one or two of the old women climbed out of the wagons and begged, "And we need some food for our children." The women and young girls wore long, colorful calico dresses. They braided bright ribbons into their long black hair. Their necklaces were strung with gold coins and glass beads, which were said to be the girls' dowries. The older the girl, the more coins on her necklace.

When the gypsy women begged, knowing that they probably would take food anyway as they went down the road, my mother gave them a loaf of bread and a dozen eggs. She told them she didn't have more. The gypsies seemed to have a philosophy that everything was held in common and that they had as much right to the produce as the farmer who raised it. They'd rob gardens, they'd dig a few potatoes, they'd take corn out of the field. If you had a garden that was a distance from the house, they'd pick the ripe vegetables and take them. If they came to a farmhouse and nobody was home, they'd go to the henhouse and gather all the eggs and catch a few chickens, and if the smokehouse door wasn't locked, they'd reach in and grab a ham or side of bacon. They'd load a sack with oats or corn for their horses and then disappear. Sometimes we wouldn't even miss what was taken, and if we did miss supplies, we knew that the gypsies had been around.

I've heard that they'd even milk a cow if they came across one in the pasture. They wouldn't milk her quite dry, so that the farmer would think that she just didn't give much milk that day. At any rate, they helped themselves quite freely to what was available. If chickens wandered off or if ducks or geese wandered off too far from the farmhouse, the gypsies had meat for the night. I don't remember anyone ever accusing them of violence. It seemed that farmers just tolerated the thievery and were glad when they were gone.

One spring they came early, before school was out for the summer. I had to walk a mile and a half to school, a mile in one direction to the crossroads by myself, then I met the other kids to walk the last half-mile together. On that particular evening, when we were coming home from school, we saw a gypsy camp down the road toward my house. Among us was a twelve-year-old boy, Warren, who always teased me. He was quite cruel to little kids, and I was only seven.

"Oh, you've got to walk by the gypsy camp," he said. "They'll get you."

"Oh no they won't. My mother says they don't bother children." I said that even though I wasn't sure she was right.

"She's just saying that, Julia, so you won't be afraid. They'll get you if they can."

After I left the other children at the crossing, I had to go up a grade, over a railroad track, down the grade, past the gypsy camp and on home. I told myself I wasn't afraid, but when I crossed over that railroad track and saw them, I was really scared. I thought that if I ran, they'd know I was afraid and they'd chase me, so I was nonchalant and brave. I walked along at a regular pace with my shoulders back and my eyes straight ahead, but as soon as I got past the camp, I broke into a run and ran all the way home.

Each evening, Mama reassured me that the gypsies would not bother me and that I was perfectly safe coming home from school, but each afternoon when I left the group, Warren told me, "Well, this is the day they get you." And I was mighty happy the day I came over the railroad track and found they'd broken camp and moved on.

I didn't see gypsies anymore that summer, but the next summer, when my two brothers and I were playing down by our machinery shed, about a hundred yards from the house and near the road, I saw a caravan approaching. We stood by the side of the road to watch until a very old woman in a buggy, the very last vehicle, called out to me. I'd been taught to be polite to old people—to all adults, in fact—so I walked over closer, within three feet of the buggy. She was trying to tell me something, but I couldn't understand what she was saying. She reached her hand out to me and I thought she was going to snatch me. I spun around, grabbed the hands of my brothers, and ran to the house. I don't know what she wanted. They went on by and we never saw them again. That was the last time I ever saw a gypsy caravan.

Protocol

A LENGTHY ARTICLE IN an issue of a national magazine told of all the protocol that goes into the planning of a White House dinner. Everything is prescribed according to pattern, from the invitation to the farewells.

What a fuss over nothing, I thought, as I read the article. I hope I never get an invitation to one. Then I remembered what it was like when I was a child on the farm and Mama invited another family for "Sunday Dinner." Talk about protocol and regulated procedure!

First came the invitation. It was oral, extended after church, for the following Sunday. Our church shared a pastor with another congregation so we only had services every other Sunday. The in-between Sundays were when we had company or went visiting.

The invitation seemed to be very offhand. While visiting after church, Mama said to Mrs. Williams, "We never seem to see you folks. How about coming to dinner next Sunday?"

Mrs. Williams replied, "Oh, Mrs. Brown, you have so much to do, what with twins and all. There are so many of us."

"That's all right, I won't go to any bother at all," Mama promised.

So it was settled. The Williamses would take dinner with us the next Sunday.

Going to no bother meant that Mama would work all week cleaning and planning. Everything got a scrubbing, even if it was already spotless. Curtains were laundered, starched, and hung. Bedspreads and braided rugs were washed. The bare-board kitchen floor, which was cleaned every day, would get a special scrubbing on Saturday. Every farm woman wanted it said of her, "You could eat off of her kitchen floor."

On Saturday, cake and cookies were baked, as well as the usual twelve or fourteen loaves of bread. Butter was churned and molded in fancy pound pats. The kitchen stove was blackened.

One knew what was happening over at the Williams home. Mrs. Williams was equally busy planning what each family member was to wear. The little girls were being shampooed and their hair put up on rags to produce curls. The children were instructed on behavior. "Be polite, eat what is given to you and don't talk too much."

On Sunday morning, Mama had us all up for breakfast at seven o'clock. She already had six pies in the oven. As soon as breakfast was over and the beds were made, all attention was on dinner. We picked garden beans and pulled the strings; we put tomatoes in the cave to cool; we brought choice pickles and preserves from the fruit cellar. Mama spread the best white linen cloth on the table. She polished cut glass bowls and hand-painted dishes and carefully placed them ready to serve the relishes and sweets.

The men never admitted to doing anything special to get ready for company, but the barnyard was neater than usual. The barn and horses could all stand inspection. A clean barn and a good farmer were synonymous.

Dress was rigidly dictated. The host family must never show off nor dress better than their guests, yet they must dress well enough to show respect for the occasion.

My father wore "mid-week-go-to-town" clothes—new overalls, a new pair of work shoes, a white shirt, but no tie. My brothers dressed much the same. Grandpa, who always went a little better dressed—as befit the dignity of being retired—wore good wool trousers, a white shirt and his best shoes. Pinned to his suspenders was his Nebraska Historical Society pin.

Mama was in the kitchen, dressed so that she could cook and serve and yet be the attractive hostess. Her white blouse trimmed with lace and tucks and navy wool skirt were pretty, but definitely second-best. Over this was tied a serviceable coverup apron which would be changed for a white one trimmed with cross-stitch just before the guests arrived.

Sunday dinner was served between twelve-thirty and one, so the Williams's carriage turned into our driveway at twelve o'clock. Everyone except Grandpa went out to the gate to greet them. My brother John stepped up and took hold of the bridles so that Mr. Williams could lay down the lines. Of course, they had driven a handsome and lively team, as was proper for visiting.

The men shook hands and Mr. Williams said, "Just tie them to the hitching rack; they're used to standing."

My father protested and insisted that the team be unhitched and put in the barn. This was the job of the older Williams boys, assisted by our hired man.

After greetings, the men and women went to the house, having admonished the boys, "Now you kids behave, keep clean, don't go far. Dinner will be ready soon. Watch your little brother and don't let him get behind the horses."

The girls hung back shyly, embarrassed, even though they saw me at school all the time.

The men stopped at the porch where Grandpa was seated in his rocking chair. After shaking hands with him, they sat down. This was an opportunity for Grandpa to say, "It's a nice day, reminds me of one day when we were crossing the plains." And he was off on one of his oft-repeated stories of the early days. Both men listened as though they'd never heard the story.

After depositing Mrs. Williams's purse and scarf in the front bedroom and putting her sleeping baby on the bed, Mama said, "I must get back to the kitchen."

Mrs. Williams offered to help, "Just tell me what to do. I know how much work it is to cook for this many."

After a bit of polite protest, Mama gave Mrs. Williams a very fancy apron, all ruffles and embroidery, carefully starched. Again a protest: "Oh, this is too fancy to wear." But she tied it on and the women went to work.

Mrs. Williams looked about, "Look at all the work you've done, and you said you wouldn't go to any bother."

"Oh, this wasn't any bother, I had to cook for the family anyway."

Mrs. Williams was assigned the job of slicing tomatoes into a cut glass bowl. "What beautiful tomatoes. Mine aren't half this large."

Last-minute work of heaping fried chicken on platters, mashing potatoes, making gravy and seasoning the three kinds of hot vegetables kept the women busy (not to mention putting cobs in the firebox and watching the big coffee pot so it wouldn't boil over).

As a big girl of six, I was on the run, fetching a basket of cobs, bringing butter and cream from the deep cave, keeping an eye on the smaller children, and making a trip to the porch to ask Grandpa to mind the baby.

Seating was very much a matter of protocol. There were five Brown children, seven Williams children, two sets of parents, Grandpa, our hired man and the Williams's hired man. Of course, he'd been invited and drove over with his single horse and buggy, as he would go see his girlfriend after dinner.

Mama supervised the seating. My father was at the head of the table and Mr. Williams at the other end. Between them was Grandpa, the two hired men and as many big boys as there were places. Another table was set in the kitchen for the Williams girls and small boys. The women ate later. I was offered a place at the children's table but declined in favor of eating later with Mama and Mrs. Williams.

After Grandpa said grace, the food was passed. In addition to the chicken, potatoes, three vegetables and sliced tomatoes, there were sliced cucumbers in sour cream, cole slaw, four kinds of pickles, and jam, preserves, piccalilli, and chili sauce.

After the usual banter of how hungry everyone was and comments like "glad the cook didn't break a leg," the conversation turned to the news. Would Bryan be elected? Why did Teddy Roosevelt buy Yellowstone Park? All that money, and so far away no one will ever see it.

The children enjoyed dinner. Mama said she remembered when she was young and got leftovers, so she made sure she had plenty of drumsticks for the children's table.

By the time the women were finished helping the children, it was time to clear the men's table and serve dessert. Cake and peaches were set on the table to be passed, along with a pitcher of thick cream. A choice of pie was offered—lemon meringue, green apple, or blackberry—huge cuts of five pieces to the pan.

Then the women cleared the table and washed some of the dishes. The small children had to be washed and put to bed for a nap. The older children, both Williams and Brown, were now allowed to take off their shoes and play barefooted.

Grandpa retired to his room to take a nap and the other men went to the shady side of the barn, sitting on their heels with their backs against the wall. By now, the conversation was business, crops, weather, the market and cattle. The men lit pipes and, with no women or kids around, a few cuss words were allowable.

The Williams's hired man left, on his way to his girlfriend's house. Our hired man went with him, as there was always a sister to visit.

It was after two before the food was warmed up for the women. This was the best part of the day for them as they could relax and engage in the woman-talk that was so scarce in their lives. The subjects were endless: gardens, sewing, fancy work, recipes, children, school and church, not to mention prices, flowers and a little gossip about who was getting married and who was having a baby.

After smoking, the men walked around the farmyard looking at pigs, calves and colts, exchanging ideas about their care. Then, they hitched a team to the spring wagon and drove out to look at the crops. The small boys went along for the ride and the older boys wandered off to climb trees and play ball.

With the dishes put away, the two women could now go to the living room. Mama brought out her latest sewing projects and materials. Dress patterns were examined and fashion was discussed. New quilts and crochet patterns were shown and admired. Mrs. Williams copied or "took off" a crochet pattern and was given a pattern-block of a quilt that she admired.

By this time, the Williams baby was ready for another nap and Grandpa was up, so he was asked to mind the baby while the women went to see the garden and chickens.

Mama took a basket and a knife with her. No guest ever went away without a gift of some kind. One always shared a garden. Mrs. Williams's tomatoes hadn't done well, so Mama told me to bring an old bucket and fill it with choice tomatoes. As the women walked through the garden, the basket was filled

with vegetables. The last stop was the flower garden where we cut an armful of dahlias, asters, and zinnias. They were then wrapped in wet newspaper and put in an old syrup pail for Mrs. Williams to take home.

By four-thirty, everyone was back at the house and ready for coffee, cake, cookies, and more pie. This was served very informally, the men and women at the table and the children eating out of hand on the porch.

The team was hitched to the carriage and good-byes and thank-yous said. Everyone knew that by six o'clock, both families would need to be in work clothes, ready to milk the cows, separate the milk, and feed the cattle. The women had to care for the little chickens, gather eggs, and take care of the milk and cream. Following this, they would serve a "bite" of supper and get things ready to wash in the morning.

All the formalities of gracious living had been met by two farm families. The memory of the day lightened the load of the next week's work. Protocol!

The Hail Storm

IT WAS SUNDAY morning, the fifth of July. An air of happiness was everywhere. Papa was down at the back lot putting canvas on the binder. Tomorrow was to be the first day of harvest. I knew he felt good about everything by the way he worked. His hat was on the very back of his head and he whistled between his teeth in a tuneless manner. Papa didn't know a note of music.

When he finished with the canvas and filled the hard-oil cups, he stood up and looked out over the valley where the best of our wheat lay golden and ready for harvest. His dark eyes looked happy, yet I felt he was close to tears.

I knew how much this harvest meant to Papa and Mama. There had been three years of drought. The year before, our farm had been hit by hog cholera which wiped out the entire lot of Poland Chinas just ready for market. Lady, a valuable brood mare and registered trotter, had scratched her shoulder on a nail and died of blood poisoning. There had been some heavy doctor bills because of Grandpa's long sick spell. Brother Willie had been to several doctors as Mama and Papa hadn't yet given up hope that some doctor somewhere could make their eldest son whole in body and mind.

Turning his gaze from the field, Papa spoke to me, "Sister, go tell Mama I'm going out to look at the wheat and I want her to go along."

On the way to the house, I passed my brothers, John and Boo, playing with our old dog Spot. They were making him some harness out of binder twine. It looked like fun.

I found Mama in the kitchen. She had a happy look. Her hair was arranged high and smooth on her head. Her apron was tied in a tight, jaunty bow and she was walking bouncy like the trotters.

"Mama," I said, "Papa is going out to look at the wheat and wants you to go along. And may I go too?"

"Why, yes," she answered, "if Grandpa will stay with the twins. They're both asleep now." I started for the door when she added, "Find John and Boo and we'll take them with us."

I found Grandpa the first place I looked. He was in his watermelon patch. Grandpa raised the best melons in the county. He sold enough each year to finance a trip back East to visit his brother. Grandpa knew a lot about plants. I'd heard Papa tell Mama that he was ahead of his time, but that didn't make much sense.

Grandpa didn't notice me. He was looking at his melons like Papa looked at the wheat. The sweat was running off his shiny bald head. I waited to see a drop run into his beard.

"Grandpa," I asked, "will you stay with the twins so I can go with Mama and Papa to see the wheat?"

His brown eyes twinkled as he looked at me, and he pulled on his beard so I knew he was going to joke. "Yes, I'll take care of the papooses." Grandpa pretended to me that the twins were Indians, and he called Rita "Nancy-Do-Little" and Raymond "Skimahorn." He took my hand and we started for the house.

"Grandpa," I asked, "this afternoon will you tell me again about the time the Indians let you go safely through the plains, even though they were on the warpath?"

He smiled and said, "This afternoon and how many more afternoons?" We stopped where the boys were still playing with Spot and took them to the house with us.

Papa had Cocoa hitched to the old buggy and Mama was ready to go. John and I rode standing in back of the seat and Willie rode up in front with Mama and Papa.

We drove down the road a half-mile to the field gate. Mama and Papa were talking about how much the wheat would yield and how long it would take to harvest it. I remember Papa saying, "There's enough wheat there to pay all our debts, and if the market holds, there might be a little left over for ourselves."

Mama was usually very talkative, but this time she just looked at Papa and smiled. We turned in at the gate and drove slowly along the edge of the field. The wheat was almost up to Cocoa's shoulders. Our southern Nebraska country was as level as a table, and we could see three of our fields, each more golden than the other. A faint breeze made the heavy heads ripple, and as we watched, I got a little dizzy. Papa stopped Cocoa at the corner of the field and turned to Mama.

"Ermie, you know every crop costs a man a year of his life, but here is one that's worth it."

Mama patted his hand before saying, "This is a year we'll never forget."

A small cloud appeared in the southwest and Papa said, "We'd best get back to the house. There might be a sprinkle in that cloud."

I've never seen a cloud darken and grow like that one did, and by the time we were back on the road, Papa was urging Cocoa into a trot. Neither Mama nor Papa mentioned the yellow tones in that cloud which meant hail, though both of them must have seen it.

We reached home and drove Cocoa into the barn. Theodore offered to unhitch so Papa could help Mama get the boys to the house. Then the storm broke. We barely made it to the porch before the rain started. Grandpa was closing windows and doors.

Moments later, the hail began. Not just a peppering of hail, but great crushing, relentless waves carried by wind and rain. Papa just stood there in the kitchen as though he couldn't move. His face was pale, his eyes stricken. Mama put her hands over her ears and ran from window to window shouting, "No, no." Nothing more, just "No, no."

I was terrified for here was something that was too much even for Mama. She went to Papa, pounding her hands on his chest, crying out, "Make it stop, Charley. Make it stop."

And stop it did, just as suddenly as it began, but too late. Within seconds, the sun was shining. We knew every stalk of wheat was pounded into the ground.

Outside we found dozens of young chickens lying on the ground. They looked dead but Mama said to bring them into the house. She started a cob fire in the kitchen range and opened the oven door to let the heat into the room. Soon we had baskets full of wet chickens near the oven. Strange to say, most of them revived, and as soon as they were dry, acted as if nothing had ever happened. It was good we had the chickens to think of that first hour after the hail.

By now, Mama's hysteria was gone but it was replaced by a dull, steady look of complete discouragement. I knew even then that Mama got much of her strength from Papa with his quiet, steady ways. But that day he had no strength or hope to give.

We couldn't eat much supper and we all went to bed early.

The next morning when I awoke and came downstairs, I'd forgotten about the hail storm until I saw Mama and Papa. Mama was getting breakfast, but she moved the pans slowly on the stove and her step had lost its bounce. Papa was standing by the door, taking short nervous puffs on his pipe. His arms looked to be too heavy, as though they were pulling his shoulders down.

Mama noticed me and tried to be cheerful. "Here is my big girl, up bright and early. Just in time to bring the butter up from the cave."

After breakfast, Mama started her washing, and I was kept busy running errands and amusing the babies. I might have been able to forget the hail if it hadn't been for Papa. He didn't even help Theodore with the chores. He just sat in the old arm rocker by the sewing machine. His eyes were open, but he didn't seem to be seeing anything. And his feet were on the floor. Unless he was sick, Papa always sat slouched down with his feet above his head. Mama had tried for years to keep him from putting his feet on her sewing machine. Sensing his pain, I kept thinking that if he would put his feet up on the sewing machine, he would feel better.

In the afternoon, Mama brought in the dry clothes and asked me to fold the diapers and the tea towels. When I finished, I found Mama and Papa sitting on the back porch. They were trying to make plans.

Papa said, "Maybe we'll have to sell out and pay the bank what we can and someday get the rest of the money for them."

Mama questioned, "And not put in any wheat? What else can we do?"

Papa sounded a little cross when he said, "You can't put in wheat without seed, and if the bank wants to, they can take everything, even the trotters."

I got up and went out to my swing to think. Maybe there was something I could do. My mind wandered. If some rich man were to come looking for a kind little girl and asking for a glass of water, I would bring it to him and he would reward me with a bag of gold. Then our troubles would be over. Or, if some robbers of long ago had hidden a can filled with money under our barn and I was able to find it, that would solve the problem.

I thought about this so long that I finally went and looked under the barn. There were no cans there, not even way back where it was dark and scary.

I heard horses coming up the road but it wasn't a rich man, just Mr. Rosier, one of our neighbors. I went to greet him, but he didn't notice me. After tying his team to the hitch rack, he went straight up to Mama and Papa. He nodded, then hesitatingly said, "I've come to tell you that the Irons baby died this afternoon."

Mama started to cry. "Poor Martha Irons. Her baby and her only boy. Do you think I should go over?"

Mr. Rosier said, "Several people are there now. I think it might be more help if you went in the morning." Turning to Papa, he added, "They'll need ice, and since you're the only one with an ice house, I'd like to take some over this evening."

"Certainly, all they want. Just glad we have it."

Papa and Mr. Rosier started making plans about who would sit up that night and the next night. I knew what "sitting up" meant. Mama had explained to me how friends took care of the dead by keeping damp cloths on their faces and having the room well-ventilated. That was why ice was helpful. Also, friends were there to help the family in any way they could. Mama told me death was sad, but nothing to fear.

Then I heard Papa say, "I'll dig the grave tomorrow after I find out where the family wants it on their lot."

Mr. Rosier turned to leave and said, "Well, I have to go to town now to get a casket and to notify Reverend Strong. I'll stop back about seven-thirty. Charlie, you and I can sit up tonight and see who wants to stay tomorrow night."

Mama added, "I'll fix some food for you to take over, and if Martha wants me to, I'll keep the two girls until after the funeral."

After Mr. Rosier left, Mama turned to Papa and said, "What have we been thinking of, Charley? All the wheat in the world isn't equal to a baby, and we have two healthy babies." She was crying a little, but I knew it was for the Irons family.

After thinking a moment, Papa nodded his head and said, "We'll make out. That wheat down in the draw was pretty green, and I think enough of it will stand up to make seed. We both know the bank has always loaned us money on our name. We never did have enough collateral to cover the loan. If they can't lend us enough to raise a crop, I can get some from my cousin Sam." He picked up his hat before adding, "Well, I must get busy so I'll be ready when Otis Rosier gets back."

Seeing me standing nearby, he said, "Sister, you can help by putting grain in the feed boxes for the horses." This was a job that was a pleasure and an honor. I started for the barn, then turned and looked at Papa and Mama. I knew that in some way they had regained their courage and that happiness would again come to Free Water Farm.

Pretend

MY ONLY PLAYMATES on the farm were my brothers, so I invented friends and events to keep from being lonely. I invented whole families. One such family was the Healeys who lived on the south bank of our fish pond. The Healey family consisted of Mr. Healey, Mrs. Healey, Florence, their seventeen-year-old daughter, Mary, their daughter who was almost my age, and the hired man. Mr. Healey was quiet and reserved and paid very little attention to me. Mrs. Healey was rather plump and rosy-cheeked and very much like my mother. She was nice to me when I came to visit. Florence didn't like Mary and me. She was inclined to yell out things like, "Don't you girls dare go in my room," or "Mother, can't you make those kids keep quiet. I can't do anything with them talking like they are."

Mary was three months younger than I and had dark hair, but not as dark as mine, and her braids weren't as long as mine. She couldn't read yet, so when I went to visit, I often took one of my story books and read aloud to her. We played with our dolls and talked. Mrs. Healey gave us a lunch of bread and butter and sugar or peanut butter and asked us to go out on the porch so we wouldn't spill anything on the kitchen floor. After I went home, I would tell my mother about my trip to the Healeys. I visited them almost every day and once even went to a party there. It was a typical country party with both grownups

and children attending. Mary and I had a great time playing
games with the children who were at the party and that was an
exciting event to tell to my mother.

One evening I came home and told my mother, "Mr. and
Mrs. Healey are real mad at their hired man."

Mama said, "Oh, they are? Why?"

"Well, it started out like this. Their dog came home from
being out in the woods, and he smelled a little bit like a skunk, so
they knew he'd gotten too close to one. Later that evening, the
hired man didn't come in for supper, so Mr. Healey went out to
see why. He found the hired man down by the barn sitting on a
box with a skunk on his lap. He was petting it. When Mr. Healey
got close, the skunk jumped down and ran into the woods and
Mr. Healey said, 'What in Sam Patch are you doing? Don't you
know it's supper time?' But when they got to the door, Mrs.
Healey wouldn't let the hired man in. She said he smelled too bad.
She gave him a towel and told him, 'You go take a bath and put
on clean clothes, then hang your dirty clothes on the wash line
and let them air there till wash day.' He did as she said but he still
smelled bad, enough that they didn't any of them enjoy supper."

Mama said, "If it had been me, I'd have done worse than
that. I'd have given him a plate and made him eat on the porch."

Shortly after that, we moved from Free Water Farm to the
Morris Farm and I never saw the Healeys again. I continued for
another year with imaginary people and events. My favorite game
was going to Paris for the fashion openings. I have no idea how I
knew so much about the Paris openings and the shows there.
Certainly my mother didn't dress on a couture level. She was a
beautiful seamstress and made all our clothes, but her only sources
of fashion were two magazines, *McCall's* and *Ladies' Home Journal.*

It was customary at that time for the buyers of the fashionable
stores and the fashion writers to go to Paris spring and fall. It may

be that one of them wrote of her experiences in one of the magazines that we got. If such an article ever appeared, I'm sure that I read it, not once, but several times.

For my trip to Paris, I had quite a few props and Mama seldom denied me anything I wanted to use. Of course, our living room was the Atlantic Ocean and I had to have a deck chair and a small table beside it. I had to have a novel, a box of bonbons and a blanket to put across my knees. The blanket was called a steamer rug. My mother's little sewing rocker with a footstool in front of it made an excellent deck chair. A wooden box made a deck table. I'd saved some corn candy and lemon drops and by putting them in an empty candy box, I had my bonbons. The lap cover was my sister's fuzzy pink crib blanket. At that time, people wore nautical dress for cruising. Fortunately I had a white middy blouse and a navy pleated skirt, so I was all set for my trip to France. Except for a few strolls up and down the deck, I spent the voyage in my deck chair with my beautiful blanket over my knees, reading and watching the waves and very daintily eating my bonbons. The crossing took up one evening of my game.

The next evening I attended the opening, and of course, I knew I had to have evening clothes. My white muslin pantywaist with lace around the neck and armholes was all right for a blouse. My mother had a dark silk half-slip with an embroidered flounce and this became my full-length skirt. My mother also had a black "kitten's ear" wool broadcloth coat with a silver grey satin lining. By turning the coat wrong side out and draping it over my shoulders, I had a full length silver cape and was properly dressed for the showing. It didn't matter that my hair was in two long braids and that I wore scuffed, high top, lace-up shoes. I was all ready to go. For the little gold chair in the salon, I brought out my mother's wicker bedroom chair. I could easily imagine it was gold.

So for this night, our living room became the designer salon. I sat on the little gold chair. Directly in front of me on the wall of our living room, was a gilded iron stairway. The models came down this stairway to a parquet platform where they made their turns and then exited.

There were thirteen or fourteen beautiful outfits in the show; however, I can remember only two of them. But I remember them so vividly that if I had the fabrics, I could cut and make them today. One was a white serge daytime dress. It had long leg-of-mutton sleeves, a surplice front blouse, and a slim skirt. A pleated Roman-striped, multicolored grosgrain ribbon went around the neck, stood up at the back and came across the surplice to the front and then down the seam to the hem of the skirt. In 1910, the newest thing was split skirts, so this skirt was split up some twelve or fourteen inches at the bottom. The model wore white kid pumps with spool-shaped Spanish heels. She had a white beaver felt hat which was draped around the brim with ribbons which matched the colored trim on the dress.

The other dress I remember was black silk — rather lightweight — with big red roses on it. The roses were satiny and slightly raised. It, too, had leg-of-mutton sleeves, only with a much larger puff at the top. The blouson had a fitted back and a blouse front. The gored skirt was full at the bottom and had a bit of drapery fourteen inches above the hem. There was a stand-up band of crushed silk around the neck, boned at the side. This dress hooked-and-eyed down the back, including the collar. The model wore black kid pumps and black gloves. She had a wide-brimmed hat made of several layers of black tulle and a rather blousy crown, surrounded by a wreath of beautiful, red silk roses. She carried a parasol of black silk with a long, slim handle of engraved silver.

In the audience was a duke and a "dukess," as I pronounced duchess, and for some reason, after the show was over, they invited everyone present to come to their palace the next night to a ball. So I was assured of another night's fun in my game.

The next night I got ready for the ball. I had to wear the same evening gown and the same cape because that's all I had, but I added gloves and a fan. It didn't matter that the gloves were a pair of my mother's with holes in the fingers and that I had to improvise the fan. I took a large square of white paper, accordion-pleated it, and fastened it together at one end with a safety pin. Then, I ran a piece of short black shoelace through the safety pin, tied a bow, and had a loop to hang the fan from my wrist, as was fashionable in those days.

Arriving at the ball, I handed a maid my cape. Almost immediately, I was dancing in the beautiful ballroom which included our whole living room. I danced fiercely and with a lot of gusto that entire evening. I even had one dance with the duke and when the evening was over, I was so tired that I didn't even argue when Mama said, "Julia, it's time to go to bed."

Harvest Help

WE WERE SEATED in a row on the edge of the kitchen porch, our bare feet on the ground. John was six, the twins, Rita and Raymond, three-and-a-half. I was eight. Papa's friend, Abe Rensler, who ran a restaurant and a free employment agency, had called to see if we needed help. We were waiting for Papa to get back from town with the two new harvest hands.

We waited and watched until Papa came back into sight and drove up the road. He turned into our drive and stopped the team near the windmill. The little kids ran down to greet Papa, yelling. I followed halfway. Being a girl and eight years old, I couldn't rush down to meet strange men.

The first man to get out of the spring wagon was fairly tall and very slender. He wore dirty bib overalls and a blue work shirt. Black hair showed beneath his black felt hat. I heard him addressed as Slim. He carried a bundle of clothing, rolled up and tied with a length of whang leather. He walked over and sat down on the platform of the windmill.

Following him was a younger man who was somewhat shorter. He too wore dirty bib overalls and his shirt had a three-cornered tear on the upper part of the left sleeve. The hole revealed a bad sunburn with large blisters. His red-brown hair was covered with a billed cap of heavy black wool. The edge of

the cap was crusted with grease from perspiration and hair oil. After giving the kids a big smile and hello, he started to help Papa unhitch. He undid the tugs and walked to the front of the team to unfasten the neck yoke. Papa called him Ralph and gave him directions.

"You can water the team and put them in the barn. I'll go put grain in the feed boxes. Billie goes in the first stall and Belle in the third one."

A few minutes later, Mama came to the door and called dinner. We children ran to the house, but I stopped in the doorway to watch as the men came in. They washed up at the wash bench on the porch and combed their hair. As they came into the kitchen, Papa introduced them to Mama.

"This is Slim and this is Ralph. Boys, this is Mrs. Brown."

Just then, Grandpa came in from the living room, so Papa reintroduced the men. Grandpa reached out to shake hands, and it was obvious the young men were a little uncomfortable. Grandpa was a little imposing with his shiny bald head and well-trimmed white beard. Nonetheless, they managed a "Pleased to meet you, Mr. Brown."

I watched everything. Slim took a modest helping of each dish. His only second helping was a piece of meat. Ralph filled his plate as high as he could without being impolite, making a well in his mashed potatoes for gravy. His second helping was just as large, and he ate five or six thick slices of homemade bread and butter. He seemed pleased when Mama cleared away the plates and served wedges of apple pie.

As was the custom, the men went out to the porch to wait until one o'clock before going to work.

"Do you boys know how to shock?" Papa asked.

"Yes," both replied. "We shocked for two weeks in Kansas before coming here."

Mama joined the men on the porch, carrying one of Papa's old work shirts and a straw hat that Grandpa sometimes wore when he hoed weeds in his watermelon patch. Approaching Ralph, she asked quietly, "Would you like a shirt? I noticed yours was torn, and this straw hat would be cooler than your cap."

Without any embarrassment, he accepted. "Thank you."

"That building by the windmill is the wash house," Mama added. "You can change in there. Just leave your shirt there for the laundry."

+ + + + +

After supper, Slim sat on the porch and smoked, but Ralph offered to help Papa with the evening chores. Regular hired men did chores, but harvest hands weren't required to do so.

However, if they worked with a team, they were expected to unharness and feed their own horses.

Rita and John tagged Papa to the barn. When Papa realized that Ralph wanted to help, he told him he could feed and water the pigs. John showed him how. Later, Papa got two milk pails and gave one to Ralph. Ralph hesitated, then said, "I don't know how to milk."

"I'll show you," said Rita, happy to oblige. She led him to a gentle, easy-to-milk cow. Putting the pail under the cow, she said, "See, you take hold tight and pull down." She squirted a stream into the pail.

Shown up by a three-year-old, Ralph failed on his first try, but was soon milking. He was slow and milked only one cow while Papa milked the other three. By the end of the week, Ralph was able to milk two cows.

On Saturday, Papa told the men, "We quit early on Saturdays and have an early supper. I'm going to town to get groceries, so you can come along. I'll come home about nine-thirty or ten; if you want to stay later, you'll have to find your own way home." Before they left, Papa gave each of them some money.

We were asleep before Papa returned. When Ralph and Slim came to breakfast, they had haircuts and were wearing new overalls and shirts.

By Tuesday, the oats were shocked and the wheat ready for heading. This job required three more men, and Mama hired a neighbor girl to help in the house. Each year, Papa observed the men at work and decided which one he would hire to plant the winter wheat. He wanted someone who was clean and pleasant, someone who didn't swear in front of the kids and wasn't afraid to work. He asked Ralph to stay on. Ralph was delighted, and we kids were really pleased. Ralph played with us, swinging the little kids over his head and showing us new games. I was too grown-up to roughhouse, but he taught me how to play checkers. He sang show songs to me, like "Wait 'Til the Sun Shines, Nellie."

After the other help left, Ralph soon settled into the farm routine. He enjoyed the work and was good to help Mama, carrying in water and cobs. In the evening, he talked to Grandpa, listening to his stories of crossing the plains. We children plied him with questions.

"Where are you from?"

When he said Omaha, we asked if it was a big city.

"Yes, pretty big."

We learned that he'd been in New Orleans and as far west as California. Ralph's mother died when he was three, and his father ten years later. He left Omaha when he was fourteen. We asked what he did each year after and why he left California.

"You may not believe this," he said, "but I got a job on a tramp steamer and was gone for two years, even went to China."

That really interested us; there were things we had to know.

"Did you eat rice? Did the men actually wear pigtails? Do you speak Chinese?"

He said that the Chinese who worked at the dock spoke some English, and the crew ate on the ship so they had American meals.

We went back to school and bragged to our friends that our hired man had been to China.

+ + + + +

Mama noticed that Ralph got no mail. She asked him if he'd let his family know where he was.

"They don't care where I am," he said. He went on to say he'd written to his sister, and she didn't answer.

"Maybe she didn't get your letter."

Every few weeks, Mama suggested he should write to his family, that they'd be worried about him.

In October, Ralph asked Papa if he could have a few days off to go to Omaha for Aksarben (Nebraska spelled backwards). Aksarben was a week-long celebration with carnivals and two parades—one was at night with lighted floats and the other was a daytime military parade.

Before going, Ralph bought a new suit and luggage. He was gone almost a week. When he returned, Mama asked if he saw his family while he was in Omaha.

"You know," he said, "I went down to the corner where my old friends had hung out, and they were still around. One of them told my brother that I was in town. My brother looked me up and said that my sister wanted to see me. Edith had written to me but she was so slow in doing it that I'd already moved on. The letter came back so they thought I might be dead. A lot of my friends who went on the bum did get killed; a lot of families gave up."

From that time on, Ralph wrote to his family about once a month.

The Blizzard

ONLY TWO GOOD crops in seven years. Those are odds that even the most courageous farmer cannot overcome. Papa and Mama decided to leave the wheat country of southern Nebraska and go across the state to the northwest Nebraska ranch country to raise cattle. Ralph moved back to Omaha. We missed him. We rented a place in Keya Paha County until we could find what we wanted for a permanent farm and ranch. The thing we liked best about going to our new home in western Nebraska was the record rainfall. After so many years of drought and hail, we knew we would love any place where it rained.

We were excited for months. Papa had been out to Keya Paha and came back with glowing reports of the hay and pasture land. He said, "The land is pretty sandy and the seasons are short, but we can raise enough corn and oats for feed, and we'll put everything we can into cattle."

"What about schools?" Mama asked.

"I couldn't find anybody who knew much about them. The people I talked to didn't have school children, but I did find out the schoolhouse is only a mile and a half from the place."

"Well," Mama said, "if they have a schoolhouse, I guess they have school."

"We'll have to have a sale," Papa said, "we'll need to raise some money, and it won't pay to ship anything but necessities."

"Do you mean sell our horses?" Mama sounded like she couldn't believe that to be possible.

"Ermie, I think you know as well as I do that we have to gamble everything on this venture. I don't see how we can take more than three horses. I figure that Billie, Belle, and Pactolena are the ones to take. I can buy range horses for a song and you know our horses will bring a mighty good price at a sale."

Mama nodded, but I knew she was thinking of her own driving horse, Cocoa. We'd raised Cocoa, and he was Mama's favorite. He was a little black trotter, a bit moody at times, but proud, and he arched his neck and pranced when he thought he had an audience. He danced and showed off on Main Street until people thought that Mama was very brave to handle him. I don't know who enjoyed it the most, Mama or Cocoa. I knew it would almost break Mama's heart to sell Cocoa, but I also knew she would never cry nor even say a word to anyone about how she felt. She was a farmer and a farmer does what she must.

+ + + + +

Days later, the sale was over and we were on the train, Mama and six of us children. Francie, the newest arrival to our family, was only a year old. The twins were five, John eight, and Willie twelve. I was ten-and-a-half and feeling very grown up. Grandpa was back in Ohio, visiting his brother. A week earlier, Papa had gone ahead in the Immigrant Car, taking our stock, farm machinery, and household goods. We were to join him in Ainsworth, the closest railroad town to our rented ranch. Our new home was twenty-five miles out across the prairie. The names all sounded so exciting—Ainsworth, Keya Paha, Nordon. The ranch was near the Rosebud Indian Reservation. We'd never seen Indians, and Papa had promised that we would see some very soon.

It had been a beautiful day and was still quite warm when our train got into Ainsworth at midnight. Papa met us and took us to a nearby hotel. We stayed in one room with two double beds. We all had much to tell him and lots of questions to ask.

"Let's get to bed," Papa said. "There's a storm predicted, and it's getting colder. Maybe we can get home ahead of the snow."

Even excited as we were, we were soon asleep. The next morning, I was the first awake. The room seemed awfully cold and I could hear the wind blowing. When I went to the window, I was greeted by a storm such as I'd never seen before.

"It's a blizzard," I said.

"Yes," Mama answered, "it's a very bad blizzard. We won't be able to start today, so why don't you go back to bed? You didn't get very much rest last night."

"May I get in your bed?" I asked. "I'm not really sleepy." As it wasn't a question that needed an answer, I climbed into the bed and listened to the storm and Mama's and Papa's conversation.

Papa was talking about the new house, and the men who had helped him haul out the household furnishings and machinery. "Two neighbors each hauled a load," he said, "but it will take two more trips with two teams to get everything out to the place."

"Where are the things stored now?" Mama asked.

"Up over the livery barn and in back of the livery hay loft, and by the way, there's a big box of bedding that I couldn't fit on the wagon. That will come in handy tomorrow to wrap the children in as it's going to be mighty cold when it stops snowing."

"What about the cattle?" Mama asked.

Papa looked worried. "They'll be all right for a while. I turned the calf in with Old Red. Our new neighbor, Bill Cannon, was coming over last night to milk Spot and to feed Pactolena. But if this storm is as bad there as it is here, he won't be able to get to our place. Why don't you get the children up and we'll go down to breakfast? Then I'll go to the livery barn to look after my team and see how bad the storm really is. It may look worse from here."

I jumped out of bed, got dressed and helped dress the twins, anxious to eat breakfast in a hotel. The dining room was cold and we waited a long time for our meal. The cook served us and said the rest of the help couldn't get through the storm. She said she lived in the hotel or we wouldn't have had anyone to get us breakfast. Mama asked for some milk for Francie and found that they only had about a cupful on hand. The cook didn't think the milkman would be able to get to town for several days. Eating breakfast in a hotel wasn't what I thought it would be, just thick pancakes and tasteless corn syrup. There was some sticky oatmeal, but only canned milk to pour over it.

After breakfast, Papa bundled up and started for the livery barn. In about ten minutes he was back, his face red and raw-looking, snow clinging to his coat and driven into his hair.

"I can't get to the barn," he said. "I came back to get more clothes and to warn you not to let the children out the door. I was afraid that Julia or John would think they could follow me. It would be death for a child to go out in this storm."

Taking off his coat, he put on a sweater and a pair of overalls over his clothes, then put on his coat again. Mama went to her suitcase and got out her big silk scarf and said, "Tie this about your face and neck."

I was surprised to see Papa do as she suggested because the scarf was pale blue, and a man just wouldn't wear that color.

"I was only a boy when the blizzard of '88 struck," Papa said, "but this one looks just like I remember that one. The only difference is, that one came without warning. I may be gone quite a while, but don't worry. I'll be near buildings all the time."

It was nearly noon when Papa got back. He carried a big armful of comforters he'd taken from the box in the livery barn.

It was so cold that night that Mama had to put comforters both under and over us. The mattresses were too thin to keep out the freezing cold. She put towels over the cracks around the windowsills. How we wished for some hot stove lids wrapped in newspaper like we always used at Free Water Farm on cold nights. Finally, Willie and Francie got in bed with Mama and Papa, and the twins, John and I curled up in the other bed. This gave us more covers. We left our wool underwear on under our nightgowns, and kept our stockings on. We were able to get to sleep and awoke the next morning, warm as toast. Even so, the room was so cold we had to dress under the covers. Downstairs wasn't much better. The hotel was low on coal, and the furnace was inadequate to heat the building in this kind of weather, no matter how much coal was used.

The blizzard still raged. After another skimpy breakfast, we sat around the lobby heat register which gave out a little heat. I found some old magazines and was perfectly happy. The twins and John were restless and the manager's wife complained to Mama, "We really don't care to take in children, especially so many in one family."

"I could put them outside," Mama said in a cool voice.

Two traveling men, also marooned, looked at each other and roared with laughter. The manager's wife left the room. She didn't say anymore to Mama, but corrected us children every time we turned around.

Papa bundled up John and took him to the barn to get a little exercise. They found a grocery store and brought back some malted milk powder, crackers, cheese and fruit to supplement the poor meals served in the dining room. Francie didn't like the malted milk, so Mama melted some chocolate candy with it and then Francie took it quite readily. The apples froze in the sack within a few hours but the crackers and cheese saved the day. All the cook had to offer that day was navy beans, rice, and coffee. Mama allowed us to have coffee for the first time in our lives.

The next morning when Papa came back from the livery barn, he brought a man whom he introduced as Sam Leighten.

"Glad to meet you, Ma'am. I'm a near neighbor to you and your husband, and we plan to travel together when we get out of here."

"How do you do, Mr. Leighten," Mama said. "How far do you live from us?"

"Oh, only about seven miles."

Mama's face dropped. Seven miles seemed like quite a distance for a near neighbor.

On the morning of the fourth day, the sun came out bright. The temperature, six below zero, seemed warm after the fifteen to thirty below we'd been suffering.

It was decided that we would leave town about ten in the morning. Mr. Leighten broke trail with his four-horse hookup, one team in front of the other, hitched to a heavy wagon. He had a load, but that made it easier to break trail. Papa wished he had brought a wagon instead of the carriage as it would have been so much warmer. We could have snuggled down in some hay in the wagon, but the day he came to meet us had been so balmy that he decided to drive the carriage. John rode with Mr. Leighten. In our carriage, the twins and Willie and I rode in the back seat while Mama, Papa and Francie rode in front. We took plenty of blankets to wrap about us and the trip started out very pleasantly.

We reached Meadville, the "Halfway House" at about one-thirty. The inn was located down in a valley on the Niobrara River, and the temperature was so warm we played while the teams rested. We had a wonderful dinner—roast beef, potatoes and gravy, string beans and pie—the first good meal we'd had in almost a week. The innkeeper's children took us down by the river and showed us a cave where horse thieves used to hide and the place where they had forded the river between Brown and Keya

Paha County so the sheriff of one county couldn't follow them into the next county. We now knew that we'd really moved west.

+ + + + +

The road climbed out of the river bottom, and we discovered we had a hard trip ahead of us. The wind came up and it was much colder. The snow drifted until there was no sign of a road and there were no more fences in the open prairie. Papa had lived in open country as a boy but I doubt he could have found his way in this weather without Mr. Leighten who knew every landmark for miles around. The snow was so deep the horses struggled, and, once, the men had to scoop a trail. The horses tired and had to rest at the top of every hill. Once Mama looked in on Francie, who was wrapped in several blankets, and couldn't wake her. She became frantic, thinking Francie had smothered. She unwrapped Francie and anxiously shook her. The baby opened one eye and said, "Bye." With a sigh of relief, Mama rewrapped her and said, "I wish the rest of us were that comfortable."

At about four that afternoon, it began to get dark and much colder. Willie shook badly and complained bitterly about the cold. I tried to keep him covered, but the twins twisted about until it was difficult to keep the blankets in place. Finally, Mama moved Rita up front with her. Then with just Raymond and Willie with me in back, I was able to tuck in the blankets quite snugly. We were all getting hungry. Willie began to get sleepy, and I was afraid he was freezing. He always chilled easily, and we seldom let him go out when it was very cold. He'd been without his thyroid extract while we were at the hotel and a few days without medicine made a lot of difference in his condition. I kept waking him and tried to feel his face to judge how cold he was, but my hands were so cold I couldn't tell. Finally, I couldn't stand it any longer and called out, "Mama, Boo's going to sleep. Do you think he's too cold?" Papa stopped the team, turned around

in the seat, and felt Willie's neck and said, "No, he's just awfully
tired. You sit in the middle, Julia, and see if you can keep the covers on him and Raymond. We are within five miles of home."

I was so tired when we reached the ranch that I thought I
couldn't stand it. Since there was no heat in the house and the
food was frozen, Papa decided to drive on to Bill Canon's, a
neighboring ranch about two miles further. Papa stopped to
check Pactolena and when he found she wasn't in the barn, he
decided Bill Canon had taken her to his place.

It was about ten-thirty when we got to Canons' ranch. They
hadn't expected us to travel and had gone to bed. Mrs. Canon
and their children, except the oldest boy, were away visiting family, so there wasn't much food ready, but it didn't take Mama
long to cook a meal. She gave Willie a glass of milk and put him
to bed. The twins had napped and were now wide awake. John
had taken a nap too, resting against Mr. Leighten on the wagon
seat. A hot fire blazed in the air-tight heater in the living room,
and I sat so close I could smell my wool dress scorching. I began
to get warm and sleepy. I dozed and lurched forward, burning
my forehead on the hot stove. It wasn't a bad burn, but I had to
cry a little. The day had been too long for a ten-year-old girl.

Mama had supper ready by then and it smelled so good, but
I was too tired to eat. Secure in the knowledge that we had heat
and food again, I crawled into bed, waiting just long enough to
ask, "Is Pactolena all right?"

"Yes," Mama said, "but she got so hungry and lonesome
during the storm that she pawed a great deep hole in her stall. If
Mr. Canon hadn't reached her when he did, she might have
died. But as it is, she's out in his barn, safe and sound. Just as
safe and sound as we are."

She kissed me and I fell asleep, knowing we had come safely
through our first western storm.

A Year in Keya Paha County

THE NEXT DAY, after our twenty-five-mile trip through deep snow and severe cold from Ainsworth to the Canon home, we were ready to go over to our new home. Mama prepared a hearty breakfast and washed the dishes. We were wrapped up and ready to go when Mr. Canon said to Mama, "Take anything you can use, because everything at your place will be frozen."

"Thank you. That would sure be a big help." Mama took a half-peck of potatoes, two onions, and a gallon of milk. Mr. Canon urged her to take several loaves of bread.

Mama said, "I did take one loaf and I can bake tomorrow."

Mr. Canon and his son, Milton, age eighteen, drove their team and wagon, following us so they could help Papa set up the stoves. About a half-mile down the road, we passed the school house that we would attend. There was smoke coming out of the chimney, so we knew school was in session. This was the first log building I had ever seen, so it was very exciting to think that this was where we would go to school. Further, we turned off the road and bumped downhill into the farmyard. The inside of the old, frame house was bitter cold.

Mr. Canon and Papa went to work setting up the stove in the kitchen. It had to be placed on an asbestos stove board as a safeguard against fire. A stove pipe and elbow connected the stove to the chimney. They chopped up a wooden packing case to start a fire. Milton took an ax and went outside to look for fuel. He discovered that the wash house behind the kitchen had a load of cobs in one end. We were glad to have the cobs, as they make a very hot, quick fire. Fortunately, one of the wagons held half a ton of lump coal that Papa bought in Ainsworth, so we had coal for a fire at night, but we had to depend on cobs and wood during the day. They set up the heating stove in the living room.

The doors of the two small bedrooms off the living room were closed to conserve heat. Mama had found a perfect place for Francie. She took her big wicker laundry basket, put a pillow in it and put Francie down in the basket, still wrapped in her blanket. The baby was content. Mama warmed up a bottle of milk and gave it her, so soon Francie was fast asleep.

Mama offered to fix lunch for Milton and Mr. Canon, but they declined and left. Mama gave us some bread and peanut butter while she and Papa drank coffee and ate sandwiches. Because it was impossible to heat the bedrooms, Mama decided to put the bedsprings and mattresses on the floor in the living room. We had quilts and blankets to make warm beds. By then, it was time for supper, so she made potato soup and opened canned peaches. We went to bed and slept snugly all night.

When we woke up the next morning, the house was already warm. Mama must have kept a fire going in the living room all night. Otherwise, it would have been unbearably cold. She fixed a hearty breakfast of biscuits and fried meat, then started unpacking the dishes, pans, and other kitchen supplies.

Farmhouses at that time didn't have any built-in cupboards. Fortunately, there was a small pantry to the left of the stove. Mama's old, oak cupboard held our dishes and silverware. The kitchen was large enough for our big extension table and the chairs around it as well as a work table. We also put a small wardrobe for coats and boots in one corner of the kitchen. Papa helped Mama set up the beds in the bedrooms. One bedroom was designated for Grandpa, but he hadn't joined us yet, so it was decided that Willie, John, and Raymond would sleep in Grandpa's bedroom. The other bedroom was for Mama and Papa, and Francie would sleep with them. At that time, when houses were cold, babies slept with their parents until they were twelve to eighteen months old. Rita and I slept in a sofa-bed in the living room. There were no closets. In each bedroom was a board nailed to the wall, fitted with a series of nails and wardrobe hooks. Anything that couldn't be folded and put in a dresser drawer or trunk was hung on these hooks. Our homes were very comfortable and quite attractive once they were arranged.

Although Papa didn't drink, he bought a case of beer for the men who moved our household goods from Ainsworth in their wagons. Evidently, they weren't very heavy drinkers, because we found a beer case with the remaining three or four bottles of beer which were frozen solid. We kids asked what was in the bottles, and when Papa said beer, we asked if we could have it.

"Sure," he said, not paying much attention.

In order to thaw the beer, we put the bottles in the reservoir which was attached to the right-hand side of the kitchen stove. The reservoir held about five gallons of water, and because there was just a sheet of iron between the oven and the reservoir, this tank always had a handy supply of warm water for household use.

When the beer was thawed out, we found the bottle opener, opened one bottle and poured the beer into a glass to taste it. It wasn't very good, so we put some sugar in it. In fact, we put quite a bit of sugar in it, about two tablespoons. It tasted better, but we still couldn't drink much, and poured it out. I don't know what happened to the last two bottles. They disappeared, and Papa never mentioned it again.

To get from the kitchen to the living room in the Keya Paha house, one had to walk across one end of the long, narrow dining room. It was inconvenient as a dining room and not nearly as nice a space to eat in as the kitchen, so Mama decided to convert that to a bedroom for us girls. She put our bed in there, and the boys continued sleeping in Grandpa's room, until he came back from his trip to Ohio, then they would sleep on the sofabed in the living room.

The house had many windows, nice porches, and trees around it. There were so many trees! After living on the high, dry plains of southern Nebraska, the trees were a delight. A large grove of tall cottonwoods grew north and west of the barn. North of the house was a long row of silver maples. We had never seen silver maples and were fascinated with their beauty. They had a regular, maple-type leaf, but smaller, and were bright, shiny green on top with silver undersides. When the wind blew, the leaves rippled with a flash of silver. We never tired of looking at those maples.

Only about six weeks of the school year remained because the term was shorter than what we were used to. On our way to school, we discovered cactus growing at the side of the path. The first time we saw them, they were about the size of a small walnut. They grew close together, an inch or two apart, and were reddish-green with many sharp spines. Some of them had small, red flowers. I had never seen cactus, so I had no idea what they were. At first, I thought they were living insects, and I was frightened. What if they jumped on us? We tried to run away, only to discover they grew everywhere on the path. But I soon discovered they were vegetation. We were careful to avoid them, but sometimes we did actually get stickers in our shoes, and Rita got one in her ankle. It festered and took two or three months to finally pop out.

There was another type of cactus we actually thought was beautiful, but we didn't know what it was called. Its round, flat pods were about two inches across, growing one on top of the other to a height of about two feet. It, too, was covered with long, sharp spines. It had a big, waxy, cream-colored bloom on the top, but it was impossible to pick it without getting pierced.

Another wonder of the prairie were the wild flowers. The only wild flowers we had known were milkweed, sunflowers, and buffalo beans. On the prairie, we found wild flowers of every variety, and we began counting them and got to fifteen. We picked the wild flowers and brought them home. Mama didn't know what most of them were called; they were different from the wild flowers she had known in Ohio. Nonetheless, we loved them all, particularly the wild roses. We put them in bowls in the house, picking fresh ones every day. I remember one flower in particular called a Pasque Flower. It was the first one to bloom in the spring, and we called it an Easter Lily. It seemed to pop right out of the ground. The four-petal bloom was purplish on the outside with a cream-colored inside and a gold stamen. Sometimes we would find them poking through the snow.

That summer, Papa felt sick a lot. He had sudden spells of intense abdominal pain. He was sick so often that Mama wouldn't let him go to the field alone. That was the first time Mama ever worked in the field. Most farm women spent some time in the fields, but Papa had always felt Mama had enough to do with the housework. That meant that I, at age ten, had to take care of the younger children and do housework while Mama was away.

While I worked inside, John was needed outside. He loved everything about the farm, especially driving horses. He was only eight years old, but he drove a team hitched to a cultivator in the summer and a mower in the fall.

Before she went to the field in the morning, Mama got everything ready for the day's meals. Then she went out while I played with the children, straightened up the house and made the beds. I peeled potatoes and put them on the stove. Some times when I'd get to playing, I'd forget to replenish the fire, and the potatoes wouldn't get done. Other times I'd put them on too early, they'd boil dry and be scorched. But Mama was patient. She explained to me how important it was that I have the table set and potatoes cooked before she came in. She cooked the meat, made gravy, and finished preparing the meal. After dinner, Mama cleared the table and laid down for a few minutes of rest. She said if she could sleep for just twenty minutes, it refreshed her. Then she went back in the field and I washed the dishes. In the evening, I had to get things prepared for the evening meal.

All afternoon, we played. We climbed up into the haymow, went hunting for wild flowers, and ran between the trees in the grove. We heard that the water table was only four feet deep, so we decided to find out if it was true. We took a post hole digger and dug down as far as we could. Using a hoe, we removed more of the sandy soil until we got down about four feet, but found no water. The next morning when we went outside, we discovered that water had seeped into the hole. It intrigued us to think the well at the windmill went down only fifteen feet where there was a constant stream of water. Later, Papa told us to fill up the hole we had dug, so a cow or horse wouldn't step in it and break its leg.

Grandpa finally joined us in April, because my parents had thought that the earlier trip from Ainsworth to our farm would be too hard on him. In the interim, he had taken a train to Columbus, Ohio, to visit his brother and returned in the milder April weather.

Papa drove the wagon to meet Grandpa's train at Ainsworth and to pick up the rest of our household goods which were stored at Ainsworth. The packing boxes contained some of Mama's best dishes and her best household linen. Unfortunately, mice had gotten into the boxes. They hadn't hurt the dishes, but they had gnawed holes in her favorite white bedspread.

Until Grandpa got home, Mama was uneasy leaving us alone when she went into the field. Even though she trusted me to take care of the little children, she felt we needed someone there for emergencies, and one such emergency had occurred. Since Francie was just a year old, I carried her every place I went. I'd set her down on the ground while I played. Once, I turned around to find Francie eating nightshade berries. I knew they were poison. Frantically, I ran my finger around her mouth and removed them. I carried Francie into the house and scribbled a note to Mama: "Come quick. Francie ate nightshade." I gave the note to Willie and told him to run it to Mama just as fast as he could. I climbed up to the top cupboard shelf and got a bottle of Syrup of Ipecac. I knew it made you throw up, and I knew Mama had it in case of croup or for when a child ate something he shouldn't. I poured some in a teaspoon and made Francie eat it. Almost immediately she threw up. Within ten minutes, Mama came rushing in. Willie went right to her. She drove the horses home as fast as they'd run.

She said, "I think she's all right, now that she's thrown up. You were smart to think of giving her Ipecac. She could have digested the berries by the time I got here." Mama kept Francie awake and watched her closely until late that evening. Then Mama knew Francie would be fine. I felt very important when Mama praised me for what I'd done, but I could tell she was relieved when Grandpa settled in.

Grandpa never worked in the field or did barn chores. He

took care of the chickens and the garden. He raised a small patch of watermelon. When we lived at the Free Water Farm near Wilcox, he raised melons to sell, and that enabled him to earn the money to go to Columbus. But there was no market in Keya Paha County, so he just raised enough melons for the family. I didn't mind helping Grandpa in the melon patch because he told me stories about the years he spent with the wagon trains hauling freight from the Missouri River to Boise, Idaho.

We didn't have rural mail delivery in Keya Paha, so we had to drive to the post office at Nordon, seven miles away, where there was a general delivery window at the post office. One day in late September, Papa was going to town with a team and wagon to get groceries and the mail. Willie, John, Raymond, and Rita went with him. When they got about halfway to Nordon, they saw a man walking towards them carrying a suitcase. It was unusual to see anyone walking in that wide, open country. The man waved his suitcase and ran toward them. They were delighted to see it was Ralph. After greetings, Ralph climbed into the wagon and went with Papa to get the mail. I was so surprised when Papa drove into the yard with Ralph riding beside him.

A few weeks later, Mr. Wheeler, a neighboring rancher, hired Ralph to help him feed cattle. Every Sunday, Ralph came home to spend the day with us. He planned to come over for Christmas that year. We watched for him all morning, but Mama couldn't wait any longer to serve dinner. We children were very disappointed.

The next morning, we were startled when Ralph walked in. I asked him, "Why didn't you come for Christmas? We waited and waited for you."

Ralph looked surprised and asked, "Isn't *this* Christmas?"

"No," Mama answered. "Yesterday was Christmas."

It turned out well, though, because Mama had cooked so much food that we could enjoy a second Christmas dinner with Ralph on the twenty-sixth.

Still curious, Mama asked Ralph, "Didn't the Wheelers have Christmas dinner yesterday?"

"No," Ralph said. "They didn't have anything special."

"What did they do for their boy? He's only about seven."

"Nothing," Ralph answered. "They didn't do anything and had no presents, either. They ignored the day."

"That poor little fella," Mama sighed.

On another Sunday, Ralph joined us at the dinner table, and again we got curious about China and began to question him.

He sighed, put his hands on the table, and pushed himself back. "Now's as good a time as any to tell you. I've never been to China."

"Why did you tell us that?" I asked him.

"Because I wanted to work for your father, and I figured that if he thought I was only sixteen, he wouldn't hire me, so I said I was eighteen. Then you kids asked so many questions about my life and I had to fill up the years, so I said I went to China."

Papa didn't say anything, but he had a sly smile on his face. I think he'd already figured that out. He'd noticed that Ralph hadn't had enough beard to need to shave when he first came to the ranch.

Ralph's job at Wheelers ended in mid-January. Papa was glad to have Ralph's help. There was a promising ranch eighteen miles away in Cherry County, and we needed help with moving. Papa and Ralph took load after load of hay and farm machinery to our new home, called Jelly Ranch after its owner, Thaddeus Jelly who had decided to retire. On March 1, one year after we settled in Keya Paha County, we moved our cattle and household goods to our new ranch home in Cherry County.

Grandpa

IN APRIL OF 1914, shortly after we moved from Keya Paha County to Cherry County, Grandpa caught cold, which was serious for a man age seventy-six. It hung on and he developed a bad cough. On a Thursday, he had a violent coughing spell. He must have broken a blood vessel. That night he started passing blood.

The next morning, Papa drove six miles to the nearest telephone to call a doctor in Valentine. The doctor didn't want to charge the dollar-per-mile fee if he couldn't help Grandpa. "I'll come out if you want me to, but there's nothing I can do. I doubt he'll survive. If he does, it wouldn't be because of anything I could do. Just keep him quiet and comfortable."

By then, Grandpa was weak and slept most of the time. Our new neighbors came to help out in the evenings and stayed up all night to let Mama and Papa get a little rest. Although we'd only lived at our ranch five weeks, the neighbors came in to help nurse Grandpa, and we'd have done the same for them.

The house was so quiet. Mama told me, "I fear we're going to lose Grandpa."

I felt very lonely and wished I could help. The younger kids didn't understand and played around as usual, but I was eleven and very fearful. I went into the living room and touched some of Grandpa's books, even turned the pages of his favorite volume of poetry. I thought about the book Grandpa had written so many years before that detailed his pioneer way of life. How I wished I had that book. He had run away from home in Ohio at age sixteen to go west. He freighted, driving oxen across the plains from Brownsville, Nebraska, to Boise, Idaho. He later homesteaded and helped build a church and a school at Wyoming, Nebraska. He submitted the book once, but the publisher returned it saying, "We get so many of these pioneer stories that we have no use for them." The book was lost.

At ten on Sunday morning, Grandpa died. Mr. Jelly and another neighbor, Mr. Bristol, washed and combed Grandpa's beard and dressed him in his best suit. They carried a door into the living room and suspended it between two chairs. A bedspread was draped over the door before they laid Grandpa on top of it. They mixed some salt peter and water in a pan and dipped soft cloths into it. They placed the cloths on Grandpa's hands and face to prevent discoloration. Papa came in and pinned the Nebraska Historical Society pin to Grandpa's lapel. To honor Grandpa, the men stayed, "sitting up" until morning. They left at daybreak.

After breakfast, Papa took a team and wagon and went to Valentine to get a casket. He also went to the doctor and reported Grandpa's death. It was the doctor's duty to file a death report at the courthouse.

Caskets were sold from a back room at the furniture store. They came complete with a pine "rough box."

Mama and I were alone most of that day. Some people stopped by briefly to bring special food such as a frosted cake or cookies. Every few hours, one of us changed the cloth on Grandpa's face. There was no horror in this; I just felt I was doing one last thing for Grandpa.

That same day, a neighbor went to Nordon to arrange for a minister to conduct the funeral the next morning. Others went to the Sparks cemetery to dig the grave. After Papa came home, some men took the casket into the living room and placed it on two chairs. After laying Grandpa in the casket, they took away the door.

The funeral was held in our living room. Only about fifteen people were present. There was no place to buy flowers, but the woman who sang brought a little bouquet of red geraniums, tied with black ribbons, and placed them in the coffin.

A spring wagon with the box bed draped with lengths of tapestry draperies served as a hearse. Our carriage, the Jelly's buggy, and two wagons made up the procession. After the grave-side words were spoken, the casket was lowered into the rough box by tying harness lines together, making two slings. Four men held the ends of the leather lines and lowered the casket. Afterward, they pulled back the lines. The lid of the rough box dropped into place. Homer Bristol climbed down into the grave and nailed the lid. Someone had to give him a hand to climb back out.

The minister chanted, "Earth to earth..." while Homer began to shovel. Mama always said the loneliest sound on earth was the first shovel of dirt falling into a grave. It was customary for the family to leave when the grave was half-filled, and so we did.

We went home to a sad and lonely house. I had no appetite for the fancy food the neighbors brought to the house, although I knew the sacrifice of sugar and flour was costly. I knew Grandpa was gone; all I had left were the memories he'd shared of his early days. These were some comfort to me.

Corsets and Lilacs

IN THE SPRING of 1914, we moved to Cherry County to live on our own ranch-farm. We'd only stayed a year in Keya Paha County, but that was long enough for us to learn that we loved ranching. All year we searched for the place we wanted as a permanent location. We found it in the Jelly Ranch.

Thaddeus Jelly and his wife had decided to retire. They had lived on the place for many years and had made it home. When it came time to retire, they found they couldn't go very far from their beloved land so they retained title to five acres at the rim of a beautiful canyon leading to the Niobrara River. Here they built a small neat house and a barn for a team and to house the model "T" Ford which they so bravely purchased. The new buildings were less than a quarter of a mile from the old existing buildings.

One day everyone except my little sister Francie and me were away from the house. I finished up the morning housework and, feeling a little lonesome, decided to walk about and enjoy the spring day. Going around to the front of the house, I was surprised to find lilacs in bloom. I thought of how Mrs. Jelly, or "Aunty Jelly" as we called her, must feel about missing the bloom of the flowers she had planted. Picking an armful, I called to Francie, "Come, Honey, let's take some flowers to Aunty Jelly."

We walked the short distance to the Jellys' new home. Aunty was laying out some new flower beds. She didn't see us until we were almost there. When she looked up, she greeted us with the smile and warmth that made everyone call her Aunty. I offered the lilacs.

"We thought you must miss your lilacs so we brought you an armful. Besides, it's a perfect day to get out of work."

Aunty thanked us and buried her face in the flowers. We were puzzled when she began to cry. "Come, dears," she said, "sit on the porch with me, and I'll tell you why I'm acting so silly."

On the way to the house she asked, "Where is your family? Are you and Francie alone?"

"Mama went to the north pasture with Papa. Ever since he started having those sudden sick spells, she doesn't let him go anyplace alone. Willie and Rita went with them. John and Raymond are herding cattle, so Francie and I are alone. I should be sewing, but I didn't feel like it. And I shouldn't say this, but I feel a little lonesome without Grandpa around."

Aunty looked at me seriously. "Of course you get lonesome. You're only eleven years old. I'm going to tell you a story about a time I was so lonesome I didn't care if I lived or died."

We reached the porch and sat on the bottom step. Aunty said, "Wait until I get some cookies for Honey and then we can visit." In a moment she was back with sugar cookies for all of us.

"Well now, I'll tell you why I cried over the lilacs. You know I do cry over them every spring. It all goes back to the year we moved here from Missouri. This ranch wasn't the home-like place it is now. Only the main part of the house, the part you use for a living room and bedroom was finished. The upstairs was an unfinished attic. I'd left a lovely, big old house back home where flowers and trees are taken for granted. Here, the only tree was that cottonwood by the old well, and it was about two feet high. There was no grass; sandburrs grew up to the door.

"You've probably heard that Thaddeus used to drink a lot with his friends. He didn't mean to and he suffered so afterwards that there was no use for me to scold him. His drinking became so bad back in Missouri that we both knew we had to do something. He heard about this place through an ad in a farm paper and asked me if I'd be willing to come west and start over. I was so anxious to help him quit drinking that I agreed without any idea of what this country was like. We sold everything to make a down payment on the place. We shipped our furniture and other necessities and bought a few cows when we got here.

"I hated leaving my mother and brothers and sisters, but it was exciting, as I had never been more than forty miles from where I was born. However, when I saw the house and bare yard, I was sick, sicker than I'd ever been in my life. Thaddeus was so happy and enthused that I tried to hide my sorrow. One day I thought he was out in the field so I indulged in a good cry, and in he walked. He got out of me just how I felt and nothing would do but we must go back to Missouri. I said, 'Thaddeus, you know why we came. We can't go back.'

"He argued that he would change for my sake. Going back would be the lesson he needed. I brought up the loss we would suffer financially. He said he would go to town the next day and see how he could work it out with the man we bought the ranch from and see about selling the cattle. I was so lonesome and discouraged, I let him tell me it would be all right.

"The next morning after he left for town, I began to see how wrong I was. I knew Thaddeus wasn't strong enough to resist his friends back home, and I realized how little we would have left if we moved again. I cried again."

All the time Aunty was telling this, she cried, and so did I, though neither one of us was really unhappy. It was the first time I ever shared such an experience through conversation. Aunty wiped her eyes on her apron and laughed.

"Well," she said, "I decided I'd do a big washing and get my mind off myself. I'd washed just a few days before so didn't have very many dirty clothes and had to dig up some extra ones. I took the bedspread off the bed and brought out my corset and some petticoats and such, and by the time I was putting them on the line, I felt pretty good. I started to hang up my corset when panic struck. I remembered that when we sold our place in Missouri and made the down payment on this ranch, Thaddeus gave me the remaining money. He didn't trust himself to carry it. I'd sewed it in my corset for safekeeping and there it had remained. Thinking that everything was gone, I started sobbing. 'We're trapped now and we can't ever go back.'

"I ripped the muslin pocket off my corset, hoping that maybe a little of the money would still be recognizable and imagine my surprise to find it all intact, very clean and bright. By then I was hysterical, laughing and crying, and at just that moment, someone rode up to the door. I couldn't tell if it was a man or a woman until she spoke. It was Lillie Warner. She was a great big woman with bright red hair and she kept it cut about three inches long. She was the first woman I'd ever seen in overalls, and she rode bareback on the ugliest, flea-bitten grey horse in the world. I looked at her and tried to smile. When she spoke, I knew she was a friend. She had a big voice, but it was kind.

"'You must be Annie Jelly. I'm Lillie Warner, your neighbor four miles south. I told Pa this morning that I figured you've been here long enough to be good and lonesome and I was coming to see you, even if my garden never got planted.'

"'Do climb down,' I invited and, before I knew it, I had told her about the money in the corset. She laughed a big laugh that shook her fat and made her face real red.

"'I had almost the same thing happen to me,' she said. 'I got mad at Pa one time and set about to wash everything and washed a pair of his overalls with his wallet in them.'

"Then I noticed that Lillie was carrying a gunnysack. She held it up. 'Here are some lilac starts,' she said. 'I divided mine this morning. Get your shovel and I'll help you plant them; just show me where. You go to the barn and get some manure with a lot of straw to mulch them.'

"I did as she told me. When we were through, we had a cup of coffee and some bread and butter. Before she left, she invited Thaddeus and me down for Sunday dinner. She's been my dearest friend ever since. These are from the same lilac bushes we planted that day, I always cry over them. I love them so, you see."

"Is that all?" I asked.

"No," Aunty laughed, and this time I could understand how she felt. "After Lillie went home, I brought in my washing, baked a pie and had a nice supper ready when Thaddeus got home.

"He came in and said, 'Annie dear, we're all set. Mr. Stageman will not only release us from our contract, but will give us back half of the money we paid down on the place. He said he could see this country was too hard for a woman like you.'

"'Why Thaddeus,' I said, 'we can't leave now. I planted lilacs today and we're invited to dinner next Sunday. I've already accepted.'

"Thaddeus grabbed me and kissed me and said, 'You goose. You goose.'

"That was the last we ever said about going back to Missouri, and you know, we love this whole place so much that we couldn't get more than a quarter mile away to retire. Now if you will just bring me some lilacs so I can have my cry each year, I'll be much obliged."

Francie and I went home. I was no longer lonely and I, too, baked a pie for my returning family.

The Stranger at the Door

DURING WARM WEATHER, the foot traveler was a common sight. They were of three general classifications: the hobo or tramp, the peddler, and the cross-country walker.

The hobo would ask for food. He offered to work for his meal, but knew that there was seldom any work he could do. Hobos traveled by stealing rides on freight trains, so they were more likely to seek food in town. If one did approach our place, Mama gave him a plate of food to eat on the porch.

The peddlers carried their merchandise in packs on their backs. All the peddlers I remember were dark-skinned and we referred to them as Armenians. Most of them carried lace and embroidery. They featured garments, dress lengths of silk, cotton or linen. On the dress lengths, a basting line indicated a blouse front, two sleeves and a front panel for a skirt, as well as collar and cuffs. These sections were hand-embroidered. The peddlers added extra yardage to complete the garment. In addition, some offered handmade lace collars and cuffs which were basted to a sheet of tissue paper. Some peddlers sold handkerchiefs and lace by the yard. Others offered costume jewelry and buttons. Only a few carried sleazy items, most of the lace and material were truly exquisite. The peddlers tried very hard to make a sale and would reduce prices if necessary. Once their business was completed, they would leave quickly, almost at a trot, and head for the next farmhouse which was a mile or two away.

The cross-country walker was well-dressed and the best groomed. He carried a case of clothes. He only stopped at meal-times, offering to pay a dollar for supper, a bed, and breakfast, or twenty-five cents for a meal only. Sometimes the cross-country walkers were interesting men.

One such man stayed the night with us once. Irvine Helms and Papa talked until late in the evening, discussing current events. Mr. Helms had particularly nice manners. The next morning after breakfast, Willie came in and warned Papa.

"That man is going up the road, hike-te-day." This was our family's word for fast. Our guest hadn't even said good-bye.

Papa got on a horse and overtook the man on the road. "I believe you forgot something, Mr. Helms."

"Oh, yes," Helms admitted. "I forgot to pay you. It was such a nice morning that when I went outside, I started walking and completely forgot."

"No," Papa said. "What you forgot to do was to thank Mrs. Brown for her hospitality. I think you'd best turn back and attend to that."

Papa rode beside him as Helms came back to thank Mama. Then he brought out a dollar and offered it.

Papa said, "No, you're a guest. Keep it." Papa said he felt it was worth a dollar to humiliate the man.

+ + + + +

After we moved to the ranch country of Western Nebraska, the peddlers came with teams and wagons. One man known as Happy Sam had a van-like wagon. A small dry goods store was contained in that space. He carried sheets and towels, summer and winter underwear for men, women and children, shirts and overalls, socks and overshoes, blankets and dress material, buttons and thread, and a tempting array of face powder, talcum powder, cold cream and perfume. Everything was high quality.

Happy Sam stopped at our place for midday dinner, and we bought a big order each time he came. Even though Sam couldn't read or write except for a few numbers, he could add up a huge order in his head and never made a mistake. If anyone charged their merchandise, Sam remembered the amount due and collected on his next trip. Sam's route started at his uncle's dry goods store in Long Pine and covered 150 miles. He always gave Mama a bottle of perfume, which she'd pass on to me.

+ + + + +

The Raleigh man, Mr. Hollingsworth, carried all kinds of patent medicine, tonic and cures for animals, and also spices and extracts. The Raleigh brand name was nationally respected for its high quality.

Mr. Hollingsworth spent the night at our place twice a year. Mama got all her spices and extracts from him. We bought cough syrup, cold remedies, and the usual medicine cabinet supplies from him. I remember two items: carbolated vaseline was the first. We called it cow salve. We used it on a cow's teats when they were raw and chapped, and even on our hands or bare feet in the summer. The other specialty item I remember was Herbed Liniment. The label said it was for man or beast. We gave it to horses for colic. For ourselves, Mama diluted it with hot water and added sugar to treat an upset stomach.

While we liked Mr. Hollingsworth very much, we'd heard he liked to tip the bottle. He must have seen the quart of Four Roses whiskey on the top pantry shelf. We used it for a medicine only.

One night when Mr. Hollingsworth was staying with us, Mama heard something in the kitchen. Putting on a robe, she went to investigate. There was Mr. Hollingsworth holding the whiskey bottle.

He blurted out, "I felt a little sick and I didn't want to bother you."

"I'm sorry," Mama said, reaching for the bottle, "but I have something much better for you. It's some of your colic liniment." That bottle was also on the pantry shelf.

Mama took a tall tumbler, put in a cup of water, some sugar and a double amount of the red-hot Herbed Liniment. He could do nothing but drink it. It must have burned clear down to his socks for an hour or more.

After he went back to bed, Mama hid the whiskey behind the flour barrel. The incident was never mentioned again, and we remained friends with Mr. Hollingsworth as long as we lived in Cherry County.

Winter

DESPITE THE BLIZZARDS and cold temperatures from November until March, we enjoyed winter at our ranch in Cherry County. One February, the thermometer never got above zero—day or night—for the entire month.

Often we'd go a week or ten days without seeing anyone except the family. Even so, we received daily mail because we lived only a mile from the Star Route between the railroad post office at Valentine and the inland town of Sparks. We took a daily newspaper and three farm magazines—the *Nebraska Farmer,* the *Iowa Homestead,* and the *Country Gentleman,* as well as the *Saturday Evening Post, McCall's, Ladies' Home Journal,* and the *Youth Companion.* Every winter we bought seven or eight books by mail-order written by popular authors such as Gene Stratton Porter, Zane Grey and Edna Ferber. We might not know what was happening just two miles down the road, but we knew what was happening all over the world.

The men had to work outside in the cold every day, but they dressed warmly. They wore long woolen underwear under heavy shirts and pants, canvas coats lined with sheepskin, and wool caps with fur earflaps. It got cold, but I never knew anyone to have frostbite.

Boys dressed like the men. Girls wore long underwear and flannel petticoats under woolen dresses. Because there was no dry cleaning, they wore long-sleeved gingham aprons over their dresses to keep them clean.

The teacher boarded with a family close to the school. The man of the house built a fire at the schoolhouse early in the morning so that it would be warm by the time school took up at nine o'clock. If the fire didn't burn well, the children kept their coats on and huddled by the stove for an hour or two.

My little brothers and sisters walked a mile and a half to school if they cut across the pasture, and almost two miles if they went around by the road. When the snow was too deep, Papa plowed a path for them. He hitched a team to a cottonwood stump and dragged it across the pasture. The stump was a satisfactory snowplow. School "kept" from nine in the morning until four in the afternoon. If it was snowing hard, it wasn't safe to cut across the pasture. The children took the long way around so that they could touch the fence wire to guide them home in a blizzard. Even the children had a fear of getting lost in a snow storm.

The evening meal was served at five o'clock when the little kids got home from school, cold and tired. There was a big Monarch cookstove in the kitchen with a firebox on the left, an oven in the center, and a reservoir on the right side that heated water for doing dishes and washing hands.

In the dining room, which was also our family room, we had what was called an airtight heater. It was a sheet-iron stove with an opening on top where we could pour in a half bushel of cobs at a time. We burned cobs all day and then before we went to bed, we banked the stove with lump coal so we had a low fire all night.

After the chores were all done, we spent lovely, long winter evenings reading or playing games such as checkers, dominoes, and cards. We talked about the news and discussed what we were reading. Mama sewed or mended and I sometimes did embroidery. About nine o'clock, Mama served apple or peach pie for dessert. Sometimes, if it was very cold, we'd have hot mush with ice cold-milk on it before we had our dessert.

Our bedrooms were unheated so we used various types of bedwarmers. One method was to fill a flour sack with ten pounds of salt, put it in the oven for a couple of hours and then put it in the middle of the bed. When my sisters and I got into the bed, we pushed it down to the bottom and put our feet against that sack of warm salt. Oh, it was cozy.

Another device was to heat bricks or flatirons and wrap them in a piece of old blanket before putting them into our beds. We slept in long flannel nightgowns between heavy wool blankets and comforters, so we slept warm and well.

In the cold of early morning, we didn't take long to dress and get downstairs where it was warm. We usually did the chores before breakfast and then the younger kids left for school.

Then Mama and I made the beds and cleaned the house. We scrubbed the kitchen and dining room every day with hot soap suds because so much mud was tracked in. There was always cooking and baking and wash day and ironing. In the afternoon, Mama sat at the sewing machine which she enjoyed very much. The men had a couple of hours to read and rest before the evening chores.

We did everything for ourselves. The girls all had long hair but the boys got home haircuts. Papa bought leather and half-soled our shoes when they were worn out.

Sometimes the men brought their work inside, mending a piece of harness or cutting wood on a sawhorse in the kitchen. We hauled in fresh water and carried out the wash water. We never wasted anything. Choice table scraps went to the dog, parings went to the chickens and the rest went to the pigs.

We separated our own milk and cream, and we used all we wanted. We stored extra cream in a ten-gallon can. When it got full, we put on a lid and sealed it, addressed it to the creamery in the city and left it beside the mailbox. The mailman took it to town and shipped it for us. The creamery tested it and sent us a check based on the pounds of butterfat it contained. The mailman brought the can back and left it at our mailbox. He charged a quarter for taking cream into town, nothing for bringing the empty can home. Ten gallons of cream brought anywhere from seven to nine dollars. We always had at least one can a week and cream checks were used for household expenses.

Under the house was a cellar with a dirt floor and walls. After the fall harvest, it was stocked for the winter. The potato bin held about forty bushels, enough for the table until the next year's crop, including seed potatoes. Beets and carrots were pulled and stored with the tops left on, laid out in a row and covered with damp sand. They stayed fresh until well after the first of the year. We always had two bushel sacks of onions. By the wall, a long wooden table was stacked with five- and ten-gallon stone jars filled with kraut, sweet pickles, dill pickles, grape jelly, mincemeat, and apple butter, lard and pork sausage. Pumpkins and cabbage were piled under the table. Our shelves were lined with big two-quart mason jars of canned peaches, pears, catsup, and over a hundred quarts of tomatoes. Hams, bacon, and fresh side pork hung from the rafters. Two barrels of winter apples purchased in town stood off to one side. These apples were individually wrapped and would keep until spring. There was also a bin of bulk apples that we used for apple pie and mincemeat.

The outside entrance to the cellar was heaped with hay and dirt for insulation. A trap door in the kitchen floor with steps going down allowed us to bring food up in the wintertime without going outside.

There was a storeroom upstairs for dried food and staples. The grocers bought cookies and crackers in twenty-gallon tin cans. After they sold the contents, they sold the cans for twenty-five cents each. We bought and filled these big cans with bushels of navy beans, brown speckled beans, lima beans and kidney beans. Dried fruit came in a wooden box lined with wax paper, ten pounds to a box. We'd have a box of prunes, raisins, and dried peaches. We had ten-pound boxes of saltines and macaroni. We also stored a case of one-hundred bars of laundry soap, as well as a twenty-four-bar case of hand soap.

We had a case of matches for lighting fires and lamps in a tin can with a lid. If a mouse got into the storeroom and chewed the head of a match, it could start a fire. Such fires were not uncommon.

Mama prided herself on setting a good table three times a day. In the wintertime, breakfast was sausage, biscuits, butter and jam, and a dish of oatmeal with cream, almost as heavy as whipping cream. If the hens were laying, we'd have bacon and eggs instead. The noon meal, which we called dinner, was soup or stew and homemade bread. Our big winter meal was supper of meat and vegetables.

We went to Valentine only four times a year, usually before school started, before Christmas, in February, and then again in the spring when we bought seeds. It was a long, hard trip and we had to bundle up to ride in the open wagon for the twenty-five miles. On the late fall trip, Mama bought Christmas presents and special treats like candy and nuts, celery and fresh fruit.

We made great plans for Christmas. Spruce and pine trees grew here and there over our canyon pasture. We took long hikes, watching for the perfect Christmas tree. We each selected our favorite tree, and the Sunday before Christmas, we all went to inspect the trees and choose the best one, then chopped it down and brought it home. We cut off the lower branches and put the trunk into a five-gallon bucket, wedged it with stone and filled the bucket with sand and water to keep the tree green. We kept it outside until Christmas Eve. Because we burned candles on it, we were very careful not to have a dry, flammable tree.

On Christmas Eve, we brought the tree into the dining room and got out our decorations. Every year, we made a few new ornaments using tin foil and colored yarn. After we went to bed, Mama decorated the tree and wrapped red tissue paper around the bucket. She put the presents under the tree and covered everything with a bed sheet.

When we came downstairs in the morning we weren't allowed to peek under the sheet. We had to wait until after breakfast and our chores were done. Then we changed into our second-best clothes and gathered in the dining room. Mama lifted off the sheet and lit the candles, as we admired the tree and enjoyed the candlelight. Then we snuffed the candles and distributed the gifts. We spent hours looking at our presents and sharing them with each other. It was just wonderful.

Then Mama and I went to work preparing Christmas dinner. We never had guests for Christmas except for Old Man Peterson. He lived on the land adjoining ours and was alone. He and his wife had immigrated from Sweden shortly after they were married. Oh, the stories he told us.

Crossing the ocean, they traveled by steerage to New York. Steerage immigrants brought their own food and bedding. They were allotted so many feet of space in the steerage area. Each person received a quart of drinking water per day. There was also a communal coal stove where they could warm up or cook food.

The trip took almost two weeks. There were two toilets, one for the men and one for the women, and neither was clean. Each family tacked up a blanket to give themselves a bit of privacy, and they slept on their feather beds. They kept their food in a box but had to be careful because if they went to sleep and left it uncovered, someone might steal it. Some immigrants didn't bring enough food; some brought food that spoiled. They could buy bread, but most of them didn't have the money. One person died and one was born on the Peterson's voyage. Mr. Peterson said that all the immigrants were overjoyed when they sighted New York.

Mr. and Mrs. Peterson took the train west to his homestead and cut pine trees to build a one-room log house. They had five children in quick succession, and Mrs. Peterson died when their twins were born. Neighbors came in and helped him with the funeral. The local women divided up his children and took them home to care for them. The next Christmas, Mr. Peterson wanted his children home for a big Swedish holiday so he baked and cooked. But when he brought them home, they didn't know him and wouldn't have anything to do with each other. They cried to go back to their foster homes. Old Man Peterson said, "I sat down and cried for an hour, but then I decided I would keep them. I raised them by myself from that time on. When I worked in the fields, I put blankets in the bottom of the wagon box and left the children there. Each time I came back around, I stopped to check on them. I was too afraid to leave them alone in the house. What if they got burned tending the fire?"

When Mr. Peterson's children finished eighth grade, they left home and got jobs. He seldom saw them after that.

The first time our family invited him for Christmas, he came freshly shaved and wearing his best suit. Papa brought out the bottle of Four Roses from the top pantry shelf. I never knew it to be served socially except when Mr. Peterson came. Papa knew that was the Old Country custom. Papa poured two glasses, and they cheered each other and drank the whiskey. Then Mr. Peterson would tell us about Sweden.

"We used to have an early supper on Christmas Eve and then we went to midnight church. Everybody was walking and greeting each other. Afterward we went home to a big feast and celebrated for a whole week."

He told us how on the day before Christmas, they put sheaves of wheat from the summer harvest on top of their houses for the birds and fed the farm animals special foods. We thought this was a great idea so we put out grain for the birds too.

We had the same menu for Christmas every year — roast chicken, dressing and gravy, mashed potatoes, buttered peas, Waldorf salad, jello with fruit in it, candied sweet potatoes, and two kinds of pie for dessert. In the center of the table were a dozen kinds of pickles and jams and homemade bread and butter. We noticed that Old Man Peterson ate with his knife, gathering up peas on his knife while he told us stories. "Back in the Old Country," he'd begin, as all the peas spilled off his knife, and he'd put the empty knife into his mouth. Mama had to kick the twins under the table to keep them from laughing.

After dinner, Mr. Peterson and Papa smoked and had another glass of whiskey. Mr. Peterson couldn't hear very well, so we all practically had to shout. It was just easier to let him do the talking. At four o'clock, Mama served coffee and fruitcake. Later, she gave him some to take home.

From Christmas until New Year's, we had plenty of fresh fruit, nuts in the shell and hard candy. School was out and we had lots of time to read and play games. The fields and canyons were beautiful in the winter covered with snow, so we went hiking or horseback riding every day. It was a great time for our family. School always started the Monday after New Year's Day and then we'd all settle back into our regular routine until spring came again.

Times of Sadness

I N THE SPRING of 1917 when we entered World War I, our nation was already deeply involved in the cause of the Allies. Ironically, Woodrow Wilson had been elected with the phrase, "He kept us out of war."

Ralph announced his intention to enlist at once. Papa asked him to wait until after harvest.

"Please, Ralph, wait. The country will need all the grain we can grow to support the war. By next year, John will be big enough to do a man's work and Raymond will be old enough to drive a team."

Ralph agreed and delayed his enlistment.

In June of 1917, we had a pleasant surprise when Mama's brother, Gus Lowther, his wife Blanche, and their three children came to visit us. They drove a Kissel Kar, a car that was only made for a few years. Gus and Mama were very close, and Papa and Uncle Gus had been good friends as young men. When they were kids they had gone to dances together and they kept up correspondence over the years. Papa was happy to see them and he was feeling pretty well at that time. Uncle Gus was thinking about moving close to us in Cherry County. Every day, they went to look at land and I took care of all the kids.

On Sunday, Uncle Gus said, "Let's go to the river and go fishing."

We'd never thought of such a thing and Papa said, "Well, I guess we could."

So we hitched up the wagon and Mama and Aunt Blanche fixed all kinds of food. There was an old abandoned house down by the river which had a cookstove in it. It was near a grassy area, so the men unhitched the horses and put them out to pasture. They fished with a seine. All these were new and wonderful experiences for us.

The men caught enough catfish to have a fish dinner the next day. Meanwhile, Mama and Aunt Blanche built up a fire in the old cookstove and fried four chickens. They'd made a big crock of potato salad and another of coleslaw. There was bread and butter, cake and pie, and half a dozen other things. They made a table out of an old door and two sawhorses, covering it with a checked tablecloth. Oh, what a feast!

Of course, we'd heard the old saying about it not being safe to go back into the water after eating, so we rested for an hour before we dove back in. Later we went home to do our chores. The next day we cooked the fish dinner.

Gus's family was with us on the Fourth of July when we burned some fireworks and ate another special dinner. Then came time for them to leave, and we were very sorry to see them go, because we'd had such a wonderful time, and Papa had felt good while they were there. But the week after they left, Papa started having attacks again. One attack was so bad that he was in terrible pain for ten or twelve hours. Afterward he said, "I give up, I'm going to Omaha for the surgery the doctor wants me to have." It was the last Thursday of July in 1917.

Mr. and Mrs. Jelly offered to drive Mama and Papa to Valentine where they took the midnight train to Omaha. After they left, Ralph came in, went to his room and laid face down on the bed. He cried and sobbed. He was crying so hard that the bed shook. When I went in and tried to comfort him, he said, "I'll never see Charley again. Oh, I'll never see him again."

I left him to cry. After Ralph got up and came out where we were, I said, "Do you really think Papa won't make it?"

He said, "Oh, he'll be fine. I just got worked up. You know my mother died in surgery. I've always been afraid of it."

We went about the work at home. Ralph and the kids were harvesting our oats field, and on this particular day I baked bread. It seems like at every crisis in my life, there was always bread to bake.

Auntie Jelly came up at three in the afternoon. Rita, Francie and I were out in back of the house. Auntie Jelly came around back, ran up, and put her arms around me. She said, "Oh, your Papa has died."

I don't know whether I fainted. I remember getting up off the ground, but I don't remember falling. Nobody said anything. I took Francie by the hand and started towards the house.

Auntie Jelly hesitated and said, "Well, maybe he didn't die, maybe he's just real sick. Your mother wired the doctor in Valentine. She told him to go down to the livery place and get someone to drive all of you to Valentine."

Mr. Jelly and the driver went out to the field and picked up Ralph and the boys. We had to get ready. Mr. Jelly would arrange with the neighbors to finish up the harvest, milk the cows, and take care of everything while we were gone. The driver waited with the limousine until we were ready. I had to hustle around and pack. Fortunately, almost everything was clean. I packed suitcases for the kids and got them washed and dressed up.

When we got into town, it was about six o'clock and we checked into a hotel. Ralph went to the depot to buy our tickets. We hadn't had any money in the house, and Ralph didn't have a checking account, so Mr. Jelly, who always kept quite a bit of cash on hand, loaned us $200. We'd heard a rumor that he loaned money out for high rates of interest, but I never found out whether that was true or not.

By the time we checked into the hotel, the stores were closed and we needed some more things. We called the owner of the department store. He understood about farm families in a situation like this. My folks had a charge account there and he knew my mother. The owner opened the door and took us into the store. We had to buy Willie a suit. All the kids had grown and we gave Willie's old suit to John, and John's suit to Raymond. A couple of the kids had to have new shoes and I needed stockings, more underwear, and some handkerchiefs.

We returned to the hotel and took the kids down to the dining room for supper. By the time we finished eating, the kids wanted to go for a walk up the street and back. Around nine-thirty, we had them lie down and rest before we caught the twelve o'clock train. What a hard trip it was. I felt so bad. I kept telling myself that Auntie was right; he was just real sick. I didn't talk to anybody and Ralph kept the little kids quiet. John looked panic-stricken and he sat by himself with his mouth in a hard line. Willie didn't seem to comprehend exactly, although when something was said about it, he'd start to cry.

When we got off the train to Omaha the next morning about eleven o'clock, we knew what had happened. Mama and Cousin Sam were there to meet us, and the minute Mama saw us, she broke down. We went into the depot, sat down and talked a while. We were going to take an afternoon train to Avoca, and we had to wait about two hours. It was a two-hour trip from Omaha to Avoca on a slow train. Mama had decided to bury Papa at the Avoca Cemetery because relatives lived nearby. She didn't know how long we'd be able to live in western Nebraska, and Avoca seemed like a better place for him to be.

While we were waiting, Mama went to the hospital and to the mortuary to take care of business. Then we left for Avoca.

When we got off the train, we had another shock—we saw them unload the casket from the express car. Mama broke down, then we all did. Although it was only about three blocks up to Cousin Sam's house, there was a carriage at the depot to meet us.

Cousin Sam had a big house. It was on a rise and you had to go up a few steps to the house. The front and back parlors opened off the front porch. The front parlor was a formal room and the back parlor, or sitting room, would be called a family room today. They had a big kitchen, dining room and a master bedroom. The house hadn't always been modern and the only bathroom was downstairs. There was a small bedroom off the kitchen and a maid's room that had been converted into a bathroom. Upstairs were four more big bedrooms.

There were some men and quite a few women waiting for us, including Cousin Lucy, her sister, Cousin May, and her daughter Maude. Some of these people I didn't know at all, but each of them had to embrace Mama and each time someone hugged her, she'd cry anew. I sat down in a big chair holding Francie in my lap. They had set out some sandwiches, cookies and something to drink for everybody in the dining room. Mama refused to eat. She didn't want anything. As I remember, I didn't take anything either, but the little kids did. Then Ralph wisely took them outside for a walk.

Shortly after that, the hearse drove up to the front of the house and someone closed the double doors between the parlors. The men rearranged the furniture and set up a trestle on which they placed the casket. Then they opened it. After they left, one of the women said to Mama, "Do you want to go in now?"

They opened the double doors. Mama went in to see Papa and I could hear her crying. Several ladies went in. A couple of them urged Mama to go upstairs and rest. Then they came out.

Someone said to me, "You can go in and see your Papa if you want to." So I went in alone. I can't describe the sensation of being there and seeing him for the first time since he'd left home. I remember that he looked nice, but he looked different, too. He had on a new suit and his hands were folded. His right hand had a big scar across the back of it from when he was a young man. He'd been running a buzz saw and reached under the blade to rake out the sawdust. A strap on his glove flew up and got caught in the blade. This jerked up his hand and cut it down to the bone. We children had always fingered and traced that scar when we sat on Papa's lap.

That scar was very much a part of him, just like somebody's eyebrows or a dimple would be. Mama told us later that when the mortuary took care of Papa, they had put his left hand over his right to cover the scar. When she'd gone in to see him, she instructed them, "I want his right hand on top. I want that scar where you can see it."

I looked at his scar and I felt that the parlor was a huge vacuum, with no air in it. I don't know how long I stood there before I went out into the back parlor. Francie had fallen asleep in a chair, and I sat down beside her.

Mama changed her dress and came downstairs. She was talking to the women when Ralph and the little kids came back. Several neighbors had come in and they had supper on the table. I remember them coaxing Mama to eat, but she couldn't. She drank a little tea, but that was about all she could take. It had been a long time since we had sat down to a good warm meal, so we children were quite hungry.

Then people began coming into the house and were taken into the parlor to see Papa. We went to bed fairly early, around eight-thirty. Mama wanted Francie to sleep with her; I guess she wanted somebody close to her. They took one bedroom, and Rita and I had another. There was another bedroom with two double beds where Ralph, Willie, John and Raymond slept. Some of the visiting cousins had the other bedroom, and of course, Cousin Sam and Cousin Lucy stayed in the downstairs master bedroom. We didn't get up very early the next morning, and our cousins had a nice breakfast fixed for us. Then we gave all the young kids a bath and dressed them.

The funeral must have been about eleven o'clock in the morning. The funeral director set up some folding chairs in the front parlor and arranged a group of chairs to one side for the family. They had to add more chairs in the back parlor and open the doors because more people came than we expected.

I don't remember anything about the funeral or what was said. I barely remember seeing the minister, almost as if I just glanced at him. I remember us climbing into the carriages and seeing the horse-drawn hearse. At that time, there were only a few motorized hearses and people didn't like them very much. There were jokes about putting the dead into a motorized hearse and rushing them to the cemetery.

The old horse-drawn hearses had a lot of dignity. They had glass sides and were draped with black velvet with cords and tassels at the corners, drawn by a black team with a black harness. Actually, the black team was used for an adult's funeral. For young people and children, the drapes in the hearse were white and a white team pulled the hearse. The horses put their feet down rhythmically, almost a cadence. Clomp, clomp, clomp. The carriages followed behind in a slow procession to the cemetery which was about a mile and a half out of town.

Mama chose a cemetery lot up on a side hill next to a lot belonging to some relatives. The grave was open. I don't remember them taking the casket out and putting it on the ground, or

anything about the service. I remember being there and that
they had a chair for Mama while the rest of us stood. I remember getting in the carriages to go back. Glimpses. That's all.

When we got back to the house, refreshments were served
and more people came to see Mama. Many were telling her
goodbye because they were going back home and wouldn't see
her again.

In the evening, I didn't go, but Cousin Sam took Mama out
to the cemetery one last time to see the grave all filled in with
the flowers arranged on top. Papa was only forty-five years old
when he died.

The next morning, we took the train to Omaha where we
had to wait for an hour. We boarded the train a little after noon
and got into Valentine around midnight. We went to a hotel
and took just one room that had two big double beds in it. We
didn't even undress when we laid down to rest. We stayed awake
until we went downstairs for breakfast at seven o'clock the next
morning when the dining room opened. Ralph went to the livery barn and again engaged a driver and car. We got home
around noon and Auntie and Mr. Jelly were there to meet us.

The Jellys told us the oats had been harvested and everything was in good condition. The kids changed into home
clothes and put away their good clothes.

I started to set the table for a midday meal, but when I got
to Papa's place, I didn't know what to do. I couldn't leave a blank
place where Papa sat. I stood there holding a pile of plates.

For some reason, my mother and father always sat side-by-
side at the table. Mama said they'd always done that even when
there was just the two of them. When she came in, I think she
guessed my quandary because she said, "Put Francie's place here."

She moved the high chair around to where Papa used to sit.
That was a wise decision because the rest of us would not have

felt comfortable if we had been moved over into Papa's place. And it would have been a terrible reminder to have just left it empty. Francie wasn't old enough to think about it, so from that time on, that was where she sat.

Mama had to make a trip to town the next day. I'll never forget how big, empty and awful that house felt. Fortunately, Auntie Jelly came back up again and spent a few minutes with me and pretty soon it was time to start the evening meal. Mama made that trip to town and back in record time; I don't know why she went.

Mama took Francie into her room that night and left Rita with me in my room. Actually Mama was very wise about how she handled things like that. But she went into a depression and it was very bad. It was the end of August. The kids started school on the first of September, while Mama got awfully cross and hard to please. She'd scold about minor things or say we did something wrong. She'd always been patient and good with us. It was doubly hard to feel so forlorn about Papa, and then feel like we'd lost her too. This lasted for quite a long time. And there was the War.

Patriotism and Beans

E WERE BROUGHT up to be patriotic, not just to act and
speak patriotically, but to feel it. Every school room
had a steel engraving of Washington and one of Mr.
Lincoln on the wall. We had special programs on their birthdays
which we took quite seriously.

On Decoration Day, as Memorial Day was called then, we
carried flowers to the cemetery to put on the graves of Civil
War soldiers. On the Fourth of July, we flew the flag. We didn't
work in the field on Independence Day unless the harvest had
been delayed and there was danger of the wheat "going down."
As the Bible says, if your ox is in the ditch, you pull him out,
even if it's Sunday.

We usually attended a community celebration on July 4th.
It was most often held in a grove, but if there were no trees on
the selected site, we ate our picnic dinners in the shade of the
wagon. We wore red, white and blue, perhaps tri-colored hair
ribbons, if that's what we had that year. The boys wore tiny flags
on their lapels or on their shirt pockets. There was always a pro-
gram, right after dinner. A hayrack served as a stage.

The first speaker was a county commissioner who talked
about how fortunate we were to be Americans. After that, we all
joined in singing a patriotic song such as "Rally Round the Flag,"
followed by a woman soloist who sang "Marching Through

Georgia." Then came the main event, the speech of a Civil War veteran. He was helped up onto the hayrack, if need be, by the men. His voice was difficult to hear as he recounted the big battles he had fought in, such as The Battle of Beaver Crossing. He ended his reminiscing with a final observation like, "Johnny Reb was as brave as any Union man. When he died, his blood was as red as that shed by our men."

After a lengthy ovation, we sang "The Star Spangled Banner." The minister offered a prayer of thanks and a wish that we'd all cherish and protect the nation that so many had died for. It was corny, and sweet, and heartfelt particularly during the war.

+ + + + +

In September, the county judge, who was also head of the Draft Board, came out to talk to Ralph.

"I heard that you plan to enlist," he said. "We want you to stay here and keep this ranch going. We need the crop. I've put you in Class Four on the draft."

Ralph felt trapped. He was disappointed, but agreed.

The war became very real to us. We read the news every noon at the dinner table. We sent to Sears for a big wool flag, four feet long. We erected a twenty-one-foot piece of water pipe for a flag pole. The flag went up every morning and came down at sunset. If we were nearby, we stood at attention for the raising and lowering. We did this despite the fact that we were the only ones who ever saw the flag ceremony.

In the summer we milked our twenty cows in the open lot; in winter we put them in the stantions of the barn. On the first really cold day that winter, John said, "I can't milk in the stantions. It makes me think about soldiers getting shot." We never knew why he felt that way, but I wondered if the dark, dank stantions reminded him of trenches.

+ + + + +

During World War I, farmers were asked to raise extra beans because they were easy to ship overseas and were a good, nourishing food. We raised several varieties for our own use, but that year we shelled an extra twenty bushels of navy beans. Because of labor shortages, the government wanted hand-sorted beans. The price paid for these was ten cents per pound, while the as-is shelled beans brought eight cents a pound.

It was worth it for us to hand-sort our beans. After supper, we'd remove our the table cloth and put the "rayo" lamp in the center of the table. We brought in a gunny sack which held a bushel of beans. Seated around the table, we poured a pint measure of beans in front of each person. Holding a pie pan under the edge of the table, we'd slide off any bad beans or bits of leaf or stem into it. The bad beans were put in an old milk pail to be fed to the pigs, while the good beans were tossed into the sack for market.

We usually picked beans from seven to nine in the evening. Then Mama served dessert and we went to bed. After several evenings of picking, it became very boring, so we decided one person should read a book aloud to the rest of us. We soon finished the new books we had so Mama suggested that we read the Bible.

It was the first time we'd read much of the Bible, even though many of our ancestors were Puritan leaders of the radical Congregationalists. In fact, my brother John's full name was Jonathan Edwards Brown after the early-day minister, which might have been enough to inspire him to attend church, except he was so shy. John truly was so shy that he couldn't even bring himself to go to church.

John wasn't the only family member named after clergy forefathers. My father, Charley, was Charles Spurgeon Brown and Willie was William Talmage Brown. Our Puritan roots were strong. My great-great grandfather (the grandfather of Jonathan Edwards) was Solomon Stoddard, whose wife, Esther, was the widow of Cotton Mather.

Solomon Stoddard was the first librarian at Harvard College. This was the connection that we preferred to claim. Hopefully, we inherited his literary bent more than his religious zeal, because during that year of sorting beans, we learned to appreciate the prose and poetry of Biblical passages as much as their messages. Believe it or not, we took turns reading, and we read from Genesis to Revelations before the beans were finished that season.

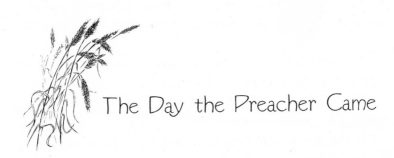

The Day the Preacher Came

THERE NEVER WAS anyone like Mama to straighten out things. Everything could be at sixes and sevens, then Mama could walk in and things would just seem to fall into place. If ever there was a time when I wished Mama was there to straighten things out, it was the time the preacher came. Of course the preacher came to our home many times before and after that day, but in my mind, that would always be, "The day the preacher came."

It was the fall after Papa died and we were getting used to the ranch being run by Mama, us kids, and Ralph. I was almost fifteen and there were four younger. John was thirteen, but a sober, manly version of thirteen. The twins, Rita and Raymond, were nine and full of the dickens, apt to get the giggles when they should be serious. Francie, or Honey, as we called her, was five. Willie was sixteen, but seemed younger. However, he was perhaps the most dependable one of us all.

The day the preacher came, Ralph and John were away hauling hay. Mama had driven thirty miles to Valentine to get winter supplies. She drove a fast team hitched to a light wagon, but wouldn't be back very early.

The grocery order was a large one as usual—five hundred pounds of flour, three hundred pounds of sugar, fifty pounds of coffee, a case of soap, and other items in proportion. While the

horses rested at the livery barn, Mama shopped for winter clothing, wool underwear, overalls, high overshoes, and mackinaws
for the boys. She bought almost the same for us girls, plus cotton and woolen material for dresses, and of course, a present for
each of us to make the day important.

While she was gone, the rest of us had taken the day rather
easy. In the morning, I baked twelve loaves of bread and cleaned
the house, but I finished early. Mama left at seven A.M., so we
had a good start on the day. We had an easily prepared dinner of
fried potatoes, bacon, sliced tomatoes, and wild plum jelly on
bread for dessert.

In the afternoon, the weather felt a little like frost, so the
twins and I gathered all the ripe tomatoes and spread horse blankets over the vines in hope of getting another picking. We had
salt cellars in our pockets and picked some late muskmelons,
eating them on the spot. How good they tasted, all ripe and
warm from the sun, in spite of the threat of frost.

We were a dirty-looking bunch when we started back to the
house. The twins had melon juice on their faces and down the
front of their overalls. I'd gathered tomatoes in my skirt and some
were over-ripe. I carried Francie part of the time and her muddy
shoes rubbed off on my dress. My long hair came loose from the
pins and blew about my face. A little honest dirt didn't worry us.
We laughed and played "I Spy." The hint might be a "C" and the
word be the cupola on the barn or a cow on the distant rim of
the canyon, or an "R" might be rhubarb. The game was going
great when Rita yelled, "Someone's driving into our place."

Raymond said, "It looks like the preacher horses." The
"preacher horses" were what we called the team our neighbor,
Mr. Bristol, loaned our current preacher each year.

In our community of scattered ranches and farms, the
church was, because of distances, poorly supported and attended.

It was kept open by a group of ladies known as the Ladies Aid Society. We shared a pastor with a church twenty miles to the east of us. He held services every third Sunday in our church and drove over and spent two or three days visiting the parish before the Sunday he gave his sermon. Since we had no phones, we never knew when he was coming. He just drove in and expected to be invited to stay overnight.

Our preachers were always one of two types, an old man who could no longer handle a larger parish, or a very young one sent out to get experience in the field. This time we had a young one, young and green, and knowing nothing of life in the country.

The preacher drove into our yard and was between us and the house, so there was no chance for me to slip by and tidy up before I greeted him. I decided to stop and welcome him and if he showed any signs of staying overnight, I'd go and clean up while he helped the twins put up his team. We didn't look up until we were within about ten feet of him. Then in a group, we looked up, smiled, and said, "Hello."

He looked at us sadly and said, "Good afternoon."

I hesitated, not knowing what to say, when Raymond saved me by saying, "Mama's gone to town."

"Ah, yes," he answered, still using the sad tone. Laying down his lines on the dashboard, he climbed out of the buggy.

Knowing that no horse should be left without a hand on the reins, Rita reached up and took hold of the bridle of the near horse. Then, in a trick typical of the twins, she turned away from the preacher to Raymond, and shaped her lips to the words, "Ah, yes."

The preacher made straight to me and held out his hand. I didn't have the courage to give him my dirty, tomato-stained hand, so I pretended not to see and shifted Francie on my arm so her skirt fell over my hands.

"Ah, Miss Brown, I want you to know you have my sympathy in this, your hour of trial." He quoted something I knew was from the Bible. I squirmed, as I'd never been called Miss Brown, and knew the twins would say, "Ah, Miss Brown," for weeks. We weren't used to formal sympathy. We all loved Papa and so had our neighbors, and they didn't talk like that.

Next he said how the Lord would take care of the widow and the orphans, "Won't he, Miss Brown?" This was too much. We weren't widows and orphans; we were a family. Orphans and widows were in books. The mothers took in washing and the children sold newspapers. They were ignorant and used bad grammar and fawned on their richer neighbors.

But angry or not, I was for the moment, head of the house and must make any guest welcome. I decided to ignore the sympathy and asked, "May we put up your team?" and added, trying to sound sincere, "Won't you stay overnight?"

He looked sad again and said, "Yes, I want to stay and give some comfort to your poor mother."

I turned to the twins and tried to give them a tough look without the preacher seeing me and said, "You kids help Reverend Mr. Royal put up his team." Turning to the preacher, I said, "If you will excuse me, I must go to the house. It's time to start supper and evening chores." And didn't that fool man leave his team and follow me to the house!

Our house had three doors, a front door that no one ever used, a side door to the dining room, and the kitchen door which we always used. This time I took him in the dining room door and asked, "Won't you sit down? Here is today's paper." I escaped to the kitchen to wash my hands.

Of course the water pail was empty and waste pail full. I emptied the waste pail, and by the time I came back, the preacher was in the kitchen. He made an ineffectual offer to get water.

"No, no," I said, "I'll get it." I went to the water barrel and found it was so low I could only dip up half a pailful. As the kitchen was the only place I had to wash, I blushed and blustered through washing my face and pinning up my hair with him looking on.

With a hurried "Excuse me," I pulled Francie upstairs and changed our dresses, then came downstairs to start supper. I wished in earnest that Mama was there to take over.

Somehow we'd relaxed too far that day. The cob basket was empty, so was the reservoir on the cook stove. The coal oil lamps were not only empty, but the flues were sooty and there wasn't enough water to get supper. The twins would be giggly and hard to get started on the chores. Scraping up what cobs were in the basket, I started a fire before I went to the door and called the twins. Dutifully they came, faking seriousness.

The preacher had parked himself between the work table and the buttery door, a place Mama would never allow anyone to sit when she was getting a meal, but what could I do or say? I had to be polite.

I gave my orders, "Raymond, you pump a barrel of water, and Rita, you get me a basket of cobs before my fire goes out."

Rita complained that cobs were Raymond's job. I told her I knew it was, but I had to have water and he was the only one who knew how to run the gasoline engine to pump it. I sent Francie with Rita. Raymond would do her job of putting the cream separator together.

I was hoping they would hurry. They still had to get the cows in and the pigs fed before Ralph and John got back with the hay. Then Willie appeared and I sent him for the cows.

Raymond loved running the gasoline engine and went right to work, but had trouble getting it to start. I had to dash down to the windmill, a city block away, to get a pail of water. On the way back, I picked up some bits of wood to keep my fire going until Rita brought the cobs. I started to fill the lamps, and in my nervousness, spilled coal oil on my clean dress. By now it was so late, I lighted the lamp with the cleanest flue for the kitchen and washed the other flue for the dining room.

Between times, I spoke a few words to the preacher who still sat by the buttery door looking sad. I made a trip to the cellar to get potatoes and some slices of ham. I peeled potatoes and tried to think of what Mama would say to the preacher. Should I tell him Mrs. Newland was ill or should I ask him about his work?

The fire was low so I didn't say a word but ran down to the lot to see why Rita wasn't back with the cobs. Rita and Francie were playing carnival. Francie was the clay baby, and Rita was trying to hit her with cobs. I was in too much of a hurry to threaten them, but they could see I was angry so they both started picking up cobs with a will. In no time, the basket was full. I returned to the house to find my fire had gone out. The grate was too hot to start a fire with coal oil, so I resorted to using paper.

Raymond was still having trouble with the gas engine so I told Rita to put the separator together. She paid no attention but stood by the sink twisting the roller towel around her hands.

I smelled smoke coming from the dining room and knew the flame had climbed and blackened my only clean flue. I was upset because I knew to start a lamp with a low flame. I went into the dining room where the preacher couldn't see me and called Rita. I knew the preacher could hear so when Rita came in, I used a sweet voice and said, "Dear, you must put the separator together." At the same time, I grabbed her by the back of the neck and squeezed until she went down on her knees.

In a sweet voice, she answered, "Okay, Julia, I'll hurry."

I went back to the kitchen and managed a few words with the preacher while I peeled potatoes. Then, just as I was putting

them on to cook, I caught a faint smell of coal oil coming from the kettle. Nothing could save the potatoes. I put them into the swill pail and went back to the cellar for more potatoes to start over again. Thunder and mud! What else could happen? I wanted to cry but didn't have time.

I knew one of Mama's ways of dressing up a meal was to make a sour cream cake and serve it warm with canned fruit. I'd been making sour cream cake since I was eight, and knew the recipe by heart, so it didn't take me long to get one in the oven. I had started frying the ham when I heard the gas engine start. A short time before, the cows had come in by themselves. Everything seemed to be under control. I hoped Mama would come before I had to serve.

As I set the table, I had to walk around the preacher's feet every trip, so I said, "I have a lamp in the other room. Wouldn't you like to look over today's paper?"

He smiled pleasantly and said, "No, I just love to watch women cook."

I wasn't a woman, and I wasn't sure I was cooking, but having no defense, I continued to walk around his feet.

I hadn't heard the hay wagon drive in, so I was surprised when John and Ralph walked in the door, giving me a teasing look as if to say, how are you and your boyfriend getting along?

Ralph was old enough to shake hands with the preacher and invite him to the barn to see if the horses were properly cared for, yet young enough to be relieved when he replied, "I'll leave that up to you. Whatever you feed them will be all right with me."

Again, I was low on cobs and asked John to get some. I knew he would be prompt, and I didn't need to worry anymore about the outside chores.

Somehow I miscalculated the firing of the range. My ham was cooked into tasteless cracklings, and I allowed my cake to rise too high in a low-temperature oven. When I opened the door to peek, the cake cracked down the center and fell flat. The tears came just as I heard the twins shout, "Mama's coming."

I left the preacher, the cake, and the ham. I ran with the others to meet Mama. All of us went, the twins yelling, "Mama, the preacher's here."

Ralph took her team when she climbed down and handed him the lines. I was crying as I told Mama how the ham was burned, the cake had fallen, and the preacher wouldn't move from the buttery door. Mama patted me and said that everything was all right. "We'll fix it. Don't worry." She indicated a box for each of us to carry to the house. The big things would go to the storeroom later.

I can't tell you why, but everything was all right from that moment on. Mama greeted the preacher, thanked him for his condolences and said, "With the children's help, I'll get along just fine."

It didn't take her but a minute to go to her room, take off her coat, and tie an apron over her town dress. John came in with the cobs. Mama started up the fire again* and told the preacher she would have to ask him to sit in the dining room while she helped me finish supper.

In only twenty minutes we sat down to a fit-for-company dinner. Some bologna from town was steamed and put on the platter with my ham. The potatoes were smoothly mashed. A sauce of lemon and cream disguised my fallen cake. Pickled peaches and jam from the cellar completed our supper.

The next day the preacher left and I had to face Ralph and the kids teasing me, but Mama was home and she didn't let it get out of hand. Besides, by then, it did seem a little funny, even to me.

Chivari

URING THE CRISIS on Jelly Ranch, Ralph and I had so much responsibility taking care of the farm, the kids and helping Mama, we became very close. We decided we wanted to be married, even though I was only sixteen years old. Ralph talked to Mama and she agreed that it would be a good thing. Ralph bought me an engagement ring, the diamond ring I've always worn. He gave it to me on November 11, 1918, the day the armistice was signed for World War I, so it's been easy to remember exactly when I got that ring.

At the time of its origin, a chivari was a mock celebration of a shotgun wedding. After a raucous serenade, the revelers would threaten to steal the bride if they weren't given a wedding feast. Sometimes they did carry away the bride, and the groom had to ransom her.

By the 1900s in Nebraska, a chivari was a noisy, but happy, way to celebrate a wedding. Friends laughingly made threats of abduction and demanded a treat.

Ralph and I drove to Valentine to be married, and we returned home the next day. Expecting a chivari that evening, Mama and Aunty Jelly baked six cakes and got out the two-gallon, blue enamel coffee pot. At seven P.M., the noise began when our friends ran around the house banging on old tubs and buckets, ringing cowbells, and shooting off blanks.

We let them have their fun for five or ten minutes before Ralph opened the door.

"Give us a treat or we'll take your bride," they shouted. When Ralph invited them in, all twenty young people put down their noisemakers and joined us to eat and talk.

After eating, they bargained for a party. Ralph promised them a dance at Sparks, a week from the next Saturday evening. Sparks was our tiny inland town. It consisted of a general store with a post office in one corner, a church, a one-room schoolhouse, one residence, and a vacant store used at no cost for community affairs. It was empty except for a big heating stove and an old piano. This was where our Wedding Dance was held.

During the next week, we cleaned the store and shaved paraffin wax with a paring knife onto the floor. The first dance would spread it. A nearby family, the Osbornes, were engaged to furnish the music. Daisy played the piano, Hank played the fiddle, and Butch had an accordion. They charged five dollars, but expected ten. On Saturday, Mama and Aunty Jelly made three big freezers of ice cream. Again, we baked cakes.

I pressed my white satin wedding dress and fussed over my hair. I was pleased to have a chance to show my friends the dress I had worked so hard to design and sew. The street-length hem was a postwar break from traditional styles. Hanging from the shoulders was a loose panel of satin with five-inch silk fringe along the lower edge. I was proud of how prettily my dress moved and shimmered when I walked.

Guests began coming to the store by seven-thirty. Single men without girlfriends came on horseback. The others drove teams and wagons. Since there weren't enough hitching racks, some men unhitched the horses and tied them to a wagon wheel.

Dancing started at eight o'clock, and by then, fifty to sixty people were present. Several brought simple wedding gifts such as tea towels, a hand-painted plate, or a crocheted doily, even though it wasn't deemed necessary. Guests of all ages danced—everyone from the ten-year-old kids to their grandparents. Among the young people were several whom neither Ralph nor I had ever met. This was considered acceptable, as long as they lived in the neighborhood. It was a community dance.

I didn't know how to dance, so I could only watch from the sidelines while my friends whirled around me. By request, the band played a few square dances, but mostly the guests danced "round dances."

Refreshments were served at ten. There was no drinking, not even Cokes. The people with children left after the refreshments were served, while the other people stayed on. At midnight, the music stopped and, with a lot of laughing and hugging, our Wedding Dance was over. Our friends departed, wishing Ralph and me much happiness.

Goody, Goody, Sunshine

IT WAS A DARK March day, cold and grey, the day of our brother's funeral. I sat at the kitchen table, pad and pencil in front of me. The minister had asked me to write a short biography to be read at the service. I wrote "William Talmage Brown, born October 14, 1900." A family name. A noble sounding name, but I'd rather have written Willie, or Boo. What should I write next? What could I write? He hadn't gone to Harvard, nor to the State University. In fact, it had taken him two years of hard work, with my constant tutoring, to master *Baldwin's First Reader*. Actually, he didn't quite finish it. When we were within two pages of the end, he turned to me and said, "Julia, I don't want to read anymore. It's too hard."

But how he loved that book. How proud he was to be able to read. On winter evenings, when the family sat around the lamp reading, he got out his book and joined us. He read a chapter or two, and just as we all did, tore a piece of newspaper to mark his place, then put the book back on the shelf. When he finished the book, Willie put it away for a while. For the next couple of weeks, he spent his evening cutting and pasting in his scrapbooks. Then he would bring out his reader again.

Boo never held public office or headed a corporation. Could I write that he could dig a very straight row in the garden? That he was gentle with little pigs and baby calves? That he never forgot to do his chores? That he was patient when herding cattle?

Could I say that his hobby was music? He loved music and spent hours playing our old Edison phonograph with its red morning-glory horn and the black, waxed cylinders. He often asked Mama to sing his favorite songs. Sometimes he played a game with her. She whistled a tune to see how long it took him to recognize it. His favorite hymn was "Nearer My God To Thee." An uncle had culled his library and sent us a box of books. Among them was a small three-by-three-inch leather-bound book with that hymn. It had beautifully printed words on heavy cream paper. Boo would turn the pages as Mama sang. I don't know if he could read it or if he just knew when to turn the page. How sad we were to hear that song at the funeral that afternoon.

I was sorry it was such a dark day. Boo loved the sunshine so much. He always felt better when he could be in the sun. When the sun came out after a spell of gloomy weather, Willie would call out, "Goody, goody, sunshine." He'd put on his boots and coat and go out to walk in the sun.

I could almost hear the neighbors saying, "They're burying the Brown boy today. Died of pneumonia. Good thing, probably. Wasn't right in the head. Terrible burden to the family all his life."

A burden? How could that sweet, gentle boy ever be a burden to anyone? We learned so much from him. Boo knew he was different but expected to be the same as other people some day. He believed since he took medicine every day, and medicine makes people well, that some day he would be well, just like all the rest of us. We never discouraged him in this thinking.

Willie also had great understanding of people. Once when he was ten years old, he went with Papa to a neighbor's on an errand. When they returned, Mama asked him if they'd gone into the house. He said, "Yes, and Mrs. Knopt gave me a cookie, but she didn't like me."

Mama asked, "But she gave you a cookie, didn't she?"

Boo answered, "Yes, she smiled here," and he pointed to his mouth, but moving his finger up to his eyes, he said, "but she was mad up here." He sensed her fear and distaste for someone who was different.

I pulled myself back to the present and simply wrote, "died March 16, 1922, survived by his mother, three sisters, and two brothers." I folded the page and carried it to the minister. Later that dark afternoon, as we stood around the open grave, I watched Mama to see how she was holding up. Her face was grey and drawn, and she leaned heavily on John's arm. I was half-listening to the familiar words, "dust to dust and ashes to ashes," when the clouds broke and the sun came streaming through. I saw Mama lift her face, smile, and murmur, "Goody, goody, sunshine."

Epilogue—1996

ALL THE PEOPLE recorded in these pages are long since dead. In the ensuing years, Ralph and I raised two sons. For forty years, I pursued a rewarding career as a couture designer, beginning in Omaha and later moving to Denver, Colorado.

In 1963, I made my first trip to Paris, and I had tickets to the fashion showing of my favorite designer, Pierre Balmain. In our cab on the way to the salon, I said to my husband, Ralph, "If we don't sit on little gold chairs, and the models don't come down a gilded iron stairway, I'll just die."

He laughed and said, "Don't expect too much."

We tendered our tickets at the door and went inside, and lo, there were the little gold chairs in a row. On the wall in front of us was a gilded staircase descending to a platform, exactly as I'd imagined it as a child at Freewater Farm. It was a beautiful show, and I enjoyed every minute of it, but today I couldn't describe a single dress from Balmain's collection. And, alas, there wasn't a single duke or "dukess" to be found in the audience.

I traveled abroad and met many extraordinary people in my life's adventures, but none were more wonderful than the people of my Nebraska youth. These are the characters and the years I can never forget.

About The Author

Born in 1902, Julia Brown Tobias was raised in rural Nebraska, where her family operated a wheat farm, raised thoroughbred trotting horses and later ranched.

After her marriage to Ralph Tobias in 1919, she moved to Omaha, where she opened her first custom clothing design shop. The fabric shortages of World War II forced her to close that shop and the family moved to Denver.

In 1954, Julia Brown Tobias reopened her couture design shop in Cherry Creek, an exclusive section of Denver, where she designed high fashion clothing until she retired in 1972. During her career as a couturiere, she also taught costume history at Arapahoe Community College, publishing a textbook in the process.

In 1992, on the occasion of her ninetieth birthday, Julie Tobias was honored for her contribution to the fashion world at at a tea held at the Brown Palace Hotel co-sponsored by the Fashion Group and the *Rocky Mountain News*. Having lost most of her sight, Julia Brown Tobias continues to write by recording on tape.

The text is composed in
twelve-point Adobe Garamond.
The display face is Lutahline
by Judith Sutcliffe: the Electronic Typographer.
The book is printed on
sixty-pound Gladtfelter Supple Opaque
by Thomson-Shore.